THE
POLITICAL
LADDER

Insider Tips on Getting a
Job in Politics

Alexandra Acker-Lyons

ACKNOWLEDGEMENTS

Thank you, first of all, to my husband and fellow (former) hack, Jonathan Lyons. He encouraged me to write this book and provided editorial assistance along the way. Most importantly, he encourages me every day in everything.

How can someone sum up the impact their parents have had on their personal and professional development? I simply could not ask for more from my parents, Sherry Nay Acker and Edward Acker, who instilled liberal values and intellectual curiosity in me from birth. I also thank my sisters, Amanda and Laurel, as well as the Lyons family, for their love and support.

I owe a huge thank you to Gayle Laakmann McDowell, author of *The Google Resume* and *Cracking the Coding Interview*, and founder of CareerCup.com. She not only helped inspire this book but walked me through the entire publishing process, providing much needed advice and friendship along the way. I would also like to thank my editor and good friend, Lauren Rubino, for her meticulous eye and perfect grammar, as well as my sister-in-law, Sara Myer, who provided a much needed final read-through.

Thank you to many, many friends and former co-workers who contributed anonymously. And, for their wonderful contributions, I sincerely thank: Christy Agner; Georgie Aguirre-Sacasa; Patrick Baskette; Mike Berkowitz; Jennie Blackton; Heather Booth; Jackie Bray; Eli Bryan Center; Amy K. Dacey; Keya Dannenbaum; Addisu Demissie; Jean Doyle; Nikki

Enfield; Rebecca Epstein; Donnie Fowler; Laura Fruge; Mag Gottlieb; Jill Habig; Jasper L. Hendricks, III; Erin Hofteig; Carrie James; Anne Johnson; Eric J. Jones; Amy Keegan; Lisa Kohnke; Justin Krebs; Paul Lhevine; Tom Manatos; Alicia Menendez; Tyler Mounsey; Tracy Nagelbush; Erik Olson; Julie Philp; Jason Cabel Roe; Glen Roth; Emmy Ruiz; Mike Shields; Jamal Simmons; Matt Singer; Jessica Smith; Hailey Snow; Michelle Study; Neera Tanden; Jay Vincent; Simone L. Ward; Nick Warshaw; Adam Weiss; CR Wooters; and Hayley Zachary. Your tips and advice make this book so much more meaningful and your friendship over the years has made my career so much more fun!

A few words about Democratic GAIN

After the 2002 elections, some very smart people got together to try and help the great unemployed masses. Led by the amazing Amy Pritchard, they put on a job fair during a snowstorm. This morphed into a full-fledged organization called Democratic GAIN. GAIN was created as the membership association for progressive political professionals, providing the support network needed to navigate this transient field.

At the height of the 2004 elections, GAIN trained thousands of people at the Democratic National Convention and cities across the country. Since then, GAIN has changed with the times to become *the* resource for politicos looking for a job and career enhancement. GAIN finds and trains political talent and matches them to the campaigns and organizations that need their expertise.

I would have had a far less successful and fulfilling career without Amy Pritchard's mentoring and support. Simone Ward was more than a boss but a friend. I worked with and wish to thank Sasha Bruce, Nikki Enfield, Eric J. Jones, Katie Fowler Monoc, Josh

ACKNOWLEDGEMENTS

Grossfeld, Staci Haag, Alexander Lewy, Sarah Scanlon, Seth Tanner, and Jennifer Waldman; many others also helped make GAIN the incredible organization it is today. Emily Lamia, my talented, tireless Deputy Director took over as Executive Director in 2011 and GAIN is reaching new heights under her fantastic leadership.

I am so proud to have been part of Democratic GAIN and I owe them a huge debt for aiding me professionally and personally. Learn more at democraticgain.org.

CONTENTS

INTRODUCTION: WHO IS THIS BOOK FOR AND HOW CAN IT HELP YOU?

Working in politics is rewarding and fulfilling, tough and exciting. You work at the epicenter of political and economic power. Decisions you make can change the course of history.

You need to love it; the lifestyle is too tough otherwise. Heather Booth, an incredible political organizer and mentor of many says, "Follow your passion. Organizing for change has so many rewards – in the change it can bring in society and in you. But the work can be so demanding that if you don't love it, over time, seek out the work you love."

Climbing the political ladder has more than its fair share of ups and downs – candidates who make you crazy, losing elections, unemployment, legislative battles that go on for years, long hours for little money, a diet of donuts and pizza. If this is starting to sound exciting, you've found the right career.

How Can I Help?

"I wish I'd known..." Friends, co-workers, mentees, people I interviewed, even political veterans all said this to me when I told them the premise of this book. I've spent much of my career helping others find jobs in politics, whether formally through two stints at Democratic GAIN, or informally as a connector and mentor. I've seen hundreds of resumes and cover letters. Through these roles and having run two national political organizations, I know what employers are looking for.

If you want to dedicate yourself to public service or work for a cause or candidate you believe in, this book is for you. Anyone who has worked in politics knows how tough it can be—both getting the job and figuring out what comes next. It's a transient field with a lot of turnover. In an industry where it's not just what you know but who you know, being a newbie can be tough and intimidating. It's important to understand all of the political opportunities before you, whether you are interested in working on campaigns for an elected official, or an organization involved with an issue you care about. Are you starting off as an entry-level staffer, coming in as an expert, or switching careers entirely? I'll address how to prepare as a college student or career switcher specifically but there are tips in here that will help anyone at any point in their career or job search. I'll walk you through how to find your first job, how to land your dream job, and everything in between.

While I've spent my career in Democratic and progressive politics, I do have friends across the aisle who added many helpful hints to this book. The hiring process and day-to-day work is surprisingly similar, aside from ideology.

Campaign veterans, consultants, Hill staffers, executives at advocacy organizations, labor organizers, lobbyists, and folks who kick butt in the states all contributed ideas and advice to this book; soak up the wisdom of the experts!

What Do I Mean By Politics?

Most people would say that politics means working on a campaign. But there's so much more – Capitol Hill and state legislative jobs, advocacy groups, labor unions and trade associations, think tanks, lobby shops, consulting firms, and local government. I'll tell you a little about each and help you decide the best path for your interests.

Here are a few things to frame your thought process going forward:

Washington, DC vs. States

While DC is the nation's capital and the center of our political universe, it's far from the only option for having a career in politics. Many politicos have spent their entire careers working in a state capital or major city. There are two schools of thought on working in DC. One says, come while you're young, develop expertise, and then move elsewhere to put your experience to use; the other says exactly the reverse—develop your expertise in a state and put it to use in DC. I know many who have followed both paths. In fact, and certainly in campaign circles, a few cycles in the field are far more important than years in DC. It's very, very hard to land a job in DC unless you live there, though. It's just too competitive and anyone there will have a leg up when an employer asks if you can come in that afternoon to interview in person.

If moving to DC isn't an option for you right now, never fear; there will be other opportunities down the line. Cutting your teeth elsewhere may be the better path in the long run. "If your goal is to make a real difference in people's lives, state and local government is a great place to work," says Matt Singer, founder of Forward Montana. "By the time I was 22, my friends and I had elected a friend to the state house, fought a successful judicial confirmation battle, won meaningful policy fights protecting rape survivors from prosecution and extending contraception equity, and remade our state's board of regents." Real world experience matters and DC is *not* the real world.

Partisan vs. Non-Partisan and Switching Sides

What do you believe and where do you fit ideologically? Many people go in and out of partisan politics, working for nonprofits, advocacy organizations or the private sector during off-cycles. This is normal and to be expected. You hone different, valuable skill sets and expand your network during these times. If you're truly dedicated to a particular issue, a career focused on the non-partisan side may be a better fit. If you're a political junkie and love the campaign life, partisan is for you.

If you do partisan work, however, you need to choose a side. Few will begrudge you a college internship with your state representative from across the aisle, but going back and forth between parties is a big no-no. Everyone's allowed their defining moment— the time or scenario that caused them to re-evaluate partisan affiliation. There are many stories of party-switchers who became successful politicians and leaders. You're allowed to do it—once. And even then it's very difficult. So, before taking a job or even embarking on your search, carefully evaluate your personal political philosophies and determine if a non-partisan job is a better fit for now or if you're a die-hard party loyalist.

You'll probably never agree with a candidate or even a single-issue advocacy organization all of the time. Don't work for someone you wouldn't vote for, but also know you don't have to agree on everything. There may also be a specific issue you feel so strongly about that you just can't compromise to work for a candidate who disagrees with you. That's fine; know your values and be honest.

Staffer to Elected Official

If your dream is to run for office one day, a career as a political staffer may be the ticket. There are plenty of other paths as well, but learning the ins and outs of campaigns and the legislative cycle will certainly give you a leg up. You'll also create valuable contacts for fundraising, endorsements, and staffing up your race. But beware the stigma of being too much of a career politician or Beltway insider.

Hacks vs. Wonks

This is like a Team Edward vs. Team Jacob scenario. You likely fall into one of two categories but may be OK playing for the other team once in a while. Political hacks – and I embrace the moniker proudly – are folks who thrive off of moving from place to place each election cycle, working on whatever campaign comes their way. The thrill of Election Day makes up for long periods of unemployment. (Recent examples of hacks include Karl Rove and David Axelrod.) Wonks, on the other hand, like to sit at a desk and think. They like debating policy questions on Saturday night and writing white papers in their spare time. (Think of John Podesta and Grover Norquist as wonk examples). President Clinton is an example of a hybrid wonk-hack; super smart but with excellent political instincts.

I firmly believe wonks should work on a campaign and hacks should sit at a desk once in a while. But if you know what motivates you, your job search and career trajectory will be that much easier.

Get the Most Out Of It

You may not read this book cover to cover. Maybe you know you want to work on a campaign and you skip to Chapter 11 for advice, and then go back to Chapters 5 and 8 as needed. Or maybe you're a college student and a newbie to this world, so you read all the way through. Either way, have at it. Take advantage of the examples and worksheets as well as the real-life quotes from political veterans. Use this book like a textbook – highlight, write notes in the margin, and flap relevant pages. I won't be offended; in fact, I'll be thrilled.

WHAT DO YOU WANT
TO BE WHEN YOU GROW UP?

Politics is a huge world and there are many possible career paths. Know thyself; not every job or path is the right fit. Here, we'll walk through my career as an example and think about some of the "big picture" questions.

My Story

So, what do you want to be when you grow up? I never really had an answer. Well, a grown-up answer; I wanted to be President and a Broadway star *at the same time* (I was quoted in my local newspaper saying as much around age seven). Throughout my career, I never had a five-year plan. I always went with whatever sounded interesting or ruled things out by process of elimination.

I grew up in a politically engaged family – not activists, but we discussed issues of the day at the dinner table. I started off collecting petition signatures for local candidates in high school. While attending SUNY-Binghamton, I became active in the College Democrats, moving up to become my campus' President, the New York State President and, during my senior year, national vice president of the College Democrats of America. This experience led to many friendships that last to this day and acquaintances with people working in politics around the country. I'll pick up the phone for anyone who knew me back then. In other words, an early start served me well, even though I didn't come from a traditionally "connected" political family.

I got my first job through a College Democrats contact. She had interned for Congresswoman Nita M. Lowey of New York and, when I graduated, told me they were looking for a staff assistant in her district office. I interviewed and got the job. Small world story #1: One of my co-workers also went to SUNY-Binghamton and was my best friend's R.A. Keep this in mind; small world stories happen a lot in politics.

Congresswoman Lowey was named the chair of the Democratic Congressional Campaign Committee in the spring of 2001, where she would lead efforts to recruit and support candidates and raise money for congressional campaigns in Washington DC. I expressed a strong interest in joining the team and moved to DC in May of 2001 with the new job title of assistant to the chairwoman. I worked very long hours for very little money, but it was an incredible opportunity. I shadowed the congresswoman to events around DC and around the country. I sat in on as many meetings as possible and kept track of her political schedule. Talk about learning by osmosis.

Then I was unemployed for seven months. Yup, seven. The 2002 elections were not kind to Democrats. Luckily, unemployment paid the rent and credit cards paid for everything else. During this time I was offered, and ultimately rejected, a job that wasn't the right fit and was a finalist for a job that I didn't get. These were tough but important lessons. It's really hard to say no to a job when you're unemployed and don't have any other prospects. But it's crucial for your long-term success and happiness; you'll be miserable in a job you don't want and it will show in your work product. And, as the song says, "You can't always get what you want." I wasn't offered a job for which I was over-qualified.

After those seven long months, I was finally offered a terrific job as the campus outreach manager for Planned Parenthood Federation of America (PPFA), one of the largest advocacy organizations on the progressive side. I used my network here, too; Congresswoman Lowey's Chief of Staff had worked for PPFA and put in a good word for me. I got to put my campus organizing skills to work for a cause I cared about. But I had never worked for a large, bureaucratic organization before and it was challenging to adapt my passion to their slower pace. It was an amazing experience though, and I was involved in planning the March for Women's Lives, creating new organizing manuals, conducting visibility during the Iowa caucuses and New Hampshire primary, and helping to set up PPFA's first-ever national field training program.

The lure of the 2004 elections couldn't keep me there and I left PPFA in May 2004 to join the John Kerry for President campaign. Small world story #2: One of my New York mentors had just been named the political director and he brought me on board as the national youth outreach director. Working at headquarters for a presidential campaign was incredible; far from glamorous but fast-paced and exciting. We thought we were going to change the world.

Then we lost. And I was physically exhausted, emotionally drained, and unemployed again. Most of my friends were, too, and we spent most of December drinking beer at 3:00 in the afternoon and going to 11 a.m. movies. But then Amy Pritchard, who I worked with closely on the campaign while she was the Political Director for the Democratic National Committee stepped in and offered me a part-time, short-term job helping to plan a job fair for Democratic GAIN. Another good rule – when you're offered a short-term job, take it; it helps pay the bills and further develops your skills and network. Even more so when a former bigwig is offering—relationships matter. Soon enough I was named the permanent training director at GAIN and helped develop big trainings for organizations like the College Democrats and a smaller night school-like series in DC.

But I was itching to do something different and interviewed for a job as the campaign manager for the National Campaign for Fair Elections at the Lawyers' Committee for Civil Rights Under Law (yes, we had a lot of trouble fitting that on a business card), where I focused on election reform. Small world story 3: my boss had gone to SUNY-Binghamton around the same time as me and also grew up with one of my co-workers from Planned Parenthood.

My interest in election reform stemmed from my experience on the Kerry campaign. Time after time, I saw how state laws were impacting students' abilities to vote, sometimes for better but often for worse. My job at the Lawyers' Committee was the first time I delved deep into policy, working with state coalitions on legislative strategy and national partners on the Election Protection program. I helped Louisiana residents vote in the first post-Katrina elections and protected the vote for the 2006 midterms.

Then I got an unexpected phone call. Simone Ward, the former executive director of the Young Democrats of America (and my former boss at Democratic GAIN) wanted to know if I'd be interested in becoming the new executive director. I had to think long and hard about this one but I interviewed and got the job. It was the most chaotic two years of my life, running the largest partisan youth organization during the 2008 election cycle. It was scary and challenging and rewarding and hard. I managed a large staff and raised over $1.5 million for our programs. I also started to do lots of media appearances, including regular segments on Fox News and CNN. Ultimately, though, I left the Young Democrats in the spring of 2009. I was leaving a good job at the height of the recession, but I was getting married and moving to Philadelphia and the timing was right.

I followed all of the steps I outline here in looking for a job in Philadelphia. I was being picky, but I met with everyone who could be helpful. Just as I was about to call around for consulting gigs, Amy called again and asked if I would be interested in returning to Democratic GAIN as executive director. I was excited by the prospect and got the job, telecommuting from Philadelphia and traveling down to DC several times per month. This situation was less than ideal, though, and I left GAIN to become a consultant at the end of 2010.

Leaving to work on my own proved helpful on many levels. It has allowed me to pursue multiple areas of concentration, expand my network and skills, and create a flexible work environment (which was particularly useful when I moved to California, where I now reside).

I still don't know what I want to be when I grow up. And that's the best part.

What do *you* want to be when you grow up? It's OK if you don't know, but the more specific you can be, the easier it will be for others to help you.

Figure Out Your Path

There are a number of factors to consider when thinking about a job in politics. Are you a believer who wants to work for the cause or candidate that inspires you most? Are you a career politico out for the long haul and looking for the best job on the best campaign? Are you putting in the long hours for a high profile job at the White House or big bucks as a consultant? Take some time to think through these questions—they'll help you later in the book.

You also need to consider whether you want to jump around or ascend the ladder. My friends, political couple Jessica Smith and

Erik Olson, are good examples. Like me, Jess jumped around from job to job, always moving up but taking on different types of political roles. Erik started as a campaign staffer to Congressman Ron Kind, and then went to work as a scheduler in the congressional office, eventually moving up the ladder over many years to become chief of staff. Both are valid paths but they're quite different and require different strategies.

There are trade-offs in every type of job, but particularly with political jobs. For instance, campaigns allow you to see results quickly and learn as you go; big organizations provide more stability and experienced leadership. Money vs. stability vs. recognition vs. rapid mobility – it all comes into play. Political operative Tyler Mounsey notes, "Political jobs are like chess. Don't just think about the current job; think about the job five years from now that this job gets you."

Not everyone has a five-year plan though. And many who do eventually get sidetracked. "I did have a five year plan; I was going to go to law school," says Amy Dacey of EMILY's List. "But sometimes, your path leads in different ways. Don't be afraid to follow it and take advantage of new opportunities." Consultant Eric Jones notes that he developed a five-year plan after working several election cycles and learning more about what he wanted to do next. "Ironically, deviating from the normal path is what allowed me to get to where I am today."

What do you need and what do you want?
Here's where you weigh your personal trade-offs.

Needs:
- Where do you want to live? Are you willing to relocate (temporarily or permanently)? Are you OK with living on a stranger's

couch or do you want a quiet, stable place to come home to at night?

- What kind of lifestyle do you want? Are you a nine-to-fiver? Do you have child or elder care to consider? Can you work unpredictable, long hours? How much do stability and work-life balance mean to you vs. prestige or money? Work environment matters.
- How much money do you need to make? We all want to make a decent salary but you should actually sit down and figure out what you need to make; that's your baseline salary. Some things, like rent if you're living in supporter housing on a campaign, may be negotiable. Have some basic numbers in mind and know the general salary levels of various jobs. Check out Chapter 7 for my salary math worksheet.

Wants:

- Do you have a dream job in mind? There are probably several entry-level and mid-level jobs that can set you out on the right path.
- How much does recognition matter? Maybe you want a prestigious title or to work for a prestigious organization. Or maybe you want a process by which your work can be recognized and rewarded.
- Do you crave more responsibility? After you have some experience under your belt, you're likely hoping to move up in the world. This may mean more responsibility in your current job, transitioning to a new position within your organization, or looking elsewhere.
- Do you need to make more money? This is a completely valid want. Politics often doesn't pay a lot and can drain your resources. A higher, more dependable salary may mean trade-offs in other areas but you can certainly make more money while fighting for the cause.

- Is there room to move up the ladder where you are? Perhaps a new title or more training? After you've been in a position or an organization for a while, you may want to consider moving on. Think about how new responsibilities, a change in salary and benefits, a new title, and office culture will impact your needs and wants.

What motivates you?

What motivates you to do this work? It's not for everyone so think it through. Is it a particular issue or ideology? Did a famous or current politician inspire you? Do you like the fast-paced nature of a campaign? The proximity to power, real or perceived? Being able to interact with voters and help shape the future? All of these are valid motivators. "Making progress is the single biggest motivator in a job – not more money or prestige," says Rebecca Epstein of The Management Center. So think long and hard about what type of work will make you happy and keep you motivated. Obama campaign staffer Emmy Ruiz says, "I also care about someone's personal motivation. Why do you want to do this work? What compelling story do you have to share to help you relate to voters?" Chapter 4 goes into more detail about types of political jobs and what to expect from each.

What are you good at?

Make a list of your skills, everything from baking to managing volunteers. Use the list here to get you started. Think about your past successes and failures and evaluate them objectively and honestly. What was your favorite job and why? Why did you dislike your last job? Are you a people person who enjoys interacting with others or do you prefer to sit at your desk and crank out reports? It helps to talk this out with a close friend or former co-worker.

Which skills describe you?

BASICS
- Organized
- Detail oriented
- Multi-tasker
- Self-starter vs. needs more direction
- Variety of projects vs. complete projects one at a time
- Time management

RELATIONAL
- Like to interact with others
- Prefer completing tasks on my own rather than in a team
- Extroverted vs. introverted
- Teacher/trainer/mentor

QUANTITATIVE
- Good at math
- Budgeting
- Excel
- Analytical

MANAGEMENT
- Hands-on vs. hands-off
- Delegate effectively
- Provide feedback

UNDER PRESSURE
- Meet deadlines
- Attack problems head-on
- Ability to prioritize
- Keeping a cool head

COMMUNICATIONS
- Writing
- Reading comprehension
- Public speaking
- Persuasive

LEADERSHIP
- Big picture thinker
- Galvanize/inspire others
- Problem-solver
- Creative

COMPUTER/ONLINE
- Outlook: Word, Excel, PowerPoint
- HTML
- Social media
- Voter contact databases
- Fundraising databases

If you're just starting out, think about what roles you'd be good at based on past experiences and your personality. I've outlined some basics in Chapter 4. Interning is a great way to try out different types of jobs or rotate throughout several roles in one organization. Not everything will be the right fit. I had a smart, hard-working friend who just didn't fit in as a legislative assistant job on the Hill. She was unhappy and it showed in her work; ultimately, she left the job rather quickly.

Narrow it Down

"Saying, 'I want to work in politics' isn't a career path," notes campaign veteran Hayley Zachary. "You need to think about what you want to do all day. This is a broad field and there are a lot of options." If you don't know what you want to do, know what you *don't* want to do. People can't help you if you only say "I want to work in politics." It's fine to say something like, "I don't want to relocate so campaigns are likely not an option" or "I don't want to fundraise or be an assistant again," which helps narrow the possibilities for people who want to help you.

The Political Ladder:
   ✓ Identify needs and wants
   ✓ Make a list of your skills

GET READY: COLLEGE STUDENTS AND CAREER SWITCHERS

Whether you're in college, a recent grad, or trying to make a career switch, there are some ins and outs to the political job hunt that you need to know.

First, politics isn't like other industries. In business, law, and other fields, job openings are posted well ahead of time, there is a formal application and interview process, and salaries and benefits fall into strict classifications by title and rank. In politics, your resume can hit someone's desk on a Wednesday, you have a phone interview on Thursday, and you're asked to show up for work in another state on Monday. Sometimes a job can be posted for a week before it's filled. Or, the job is never even posted and the person hiring just sends a discreet email to a few colleagues.

This is why breaking into the field can be so difficult. You need to know the people in the know and be ready to jump on an opportunity at a moment's notice.

But, you ask, if I'm still in college or working 100 hours a week as a medical assistant, how can I possibly get to know people in the know? How can I best prepare myself for these mythical opportunities?

If You Are Still In College

People generally enter the political sphere when they get the bug in college or shortly thereafter. Maybe you were inspired by a local issue, a national candidate, or have strong opinions about national security. Or maybe you were always a political dork, like me. Either way, college is a great place to get your start.

Major, minor

Let's start with the obvious: your major and course work. You don't have to be a political science or government major. Or international affairs, history, or economics. In fact, sometimes an off the beaten path major can be a huge help. An English major is likely a great writer. Someone with a science or engineering background may look at problems differently and find creative solutions. And a business degree brings a whole different skill set to the table, including management and logistics experience that will likely prove very valuable.

If you're majoring in biology because Mom still thinks you're going to be a doctor or accounting so you always have something to fall back on, that's fine. You should, however, get a minor in a relevant area.

No matter what your major or minor, take a course in economics. I managed, somehow, to be a poli sci major without taking any econ classes (I was scared of math). It's my single biggest regret as an undergrad. I married an econ major and can ask silly questions like, "Honey, what's a derivative?" without feeling like too big an idiot. Unless this is also your life plan, save yourself the pain. Economics is central to everything in politics and a basic understanding will serve you well. Every policy, from a tax break to a health care reform bill, requires a budget allocation, built upon economic analysis. If you don't like the intro microeconomics course, take a political economy class instead, if one is offered.

Don't get me wrong—I got a lot out of being a political science major. I took courses about campaigns, interest groups, international relations, Congress, and political theory. All taught me important information that I have put to use, but learning this stuff in the real world in addition to class is much more valuable. So, don't sweat it too much if you don't take that senior seminar on "The Executive Branch."

We Don't Care That You Went to Harvard.
Except When We Do.

Generally speaking, people don't care where you went to college. Or that you went to college. Or that you graduated. Many a successful politico has come up a few credits short.

So putting Harvard or Oberlin or wherever at the top of your resume won't get you much. Elite schools may help you get in the door, but so will your skills and experience.

All you state school grads like me can breathe a sigh of relief. In fact, I'm more likely to hire a scrappy state school kid who worked his way through school than a 3.9 GPA from an Ivy. You learn more by doing.

Here's when we care if you went to Harvard: when we did. Or our boss did. Or we want to be able to say, "Our new staff assistant, Jill, went to Harvard." It's much more about us than you. Even still, attitude goes a long way. As in, don't have one just because you went to Harvard or Yale (or worse, you say things like, "I went to school in New Haven"). You need to know your place; you're not going to write policy right out of school. Dust up on copy machine maintenance and you'll do just fine.

Unless you're a wonk applying for a wonky job, where you went to school is an interview talking point and nothing more. Use your specific experiences while at school or summer jobs to tell the real story about who you are.

A Few Words About Your GPA

I wish someone had told me this before I studied so much: your GPA doesn't really matter. Simone L. Ward, who has worked for campaigns, party committees, and nonprofits says, "I've never once been asked to provide transcripts or a copy of my diploma. Politics is an industry where who you know is important, not what you studied in a book." Your GPA only matters if you know you want to go to graduate or law school. And I mean you *know*—like it's always been your dream to have a master's in public health or attend law school and become a federal judge.

However, a great GPA can make you stand out and help you land the interview. We'll take another look if you attended a less than stellar school but graduated with honors, or if you have a great story to tell about discovering your passion and getting high marks within your major (especially if those freshman year grades lowered your overall GPA). But if you're applying for wonky jobs, a great GPA is par for the course and won't get you the job.

Laudatory recommendations from professors don't hurt either. Developing and maintaining a good relationship with a professor or two is helpful as a reference if you don't have many professional references and as a future recommendation for grad or law school.

Here's the dirty little secret of politics though: many of the best folks didn't even graduate. We all know about Bill Gates and Mark Zuckerberg but famous politicos like Karl Rove never finished their degrees. Neither did many of my friends and former employees. Even when a job description says "Bachelor's degree required" it likely counts just as much if you can prove your qualifications in other ways. Don't tell your mom that this came from me, but if you put off school to work on a campaign—especially a presidential race—and never go back, it probably won't have serious repercussions on your career. There's always another campaign though, so finish school!

Jamal Simmons, a campaign and communications expert, started off as a volunteer on the Clinton campaign in college and then got a paid gig at the Arkansas headquarters. He took time off from school to work on the general election and then went back for one last semester to finish his degree. A job at the White House was waiting for him when he graduated.

Make Your Mark

There are plenty of ways to make your mark, besides course work and your GPA. Becoming active in or starting a political organization on your campus is a great way to get your feet wet. I started off in the College Democrats, and learned organizing basics, held policy debates, and hobbed nobbed with the Broome County, NY, political "elite." I attended events when candidates came through town, and met people like my political hero Geraldine Ferraro, Senator Chuck Schumer, and First Lady Hillary Clinton. I became active in the state and then national College Democrats, making friends and key contacts that last to this day. My exposure to party politics while still in college was absolutely critical to my future success.

If you're passionate about a particular issue, maybe that's the way to distinguish yourself. Volunteer at your local homeless advocacy organization or Chamber of Commerce. Write for the newspaper or a campus journal (just remember that anything you write is part of your permanent record). Did you organize a major charity fundraiser or a protest over raising student fees? Volunteer at a nursing home or mentor inner city kids? Any of these or similar activities are a great way to make your resume stand out and give you a story to tell in your cover letters and interviews. Not all extracurricular activities are created equal though; make sure you show a true commitment to one or two key things rather than spreading yourself too thin.

The Real World

Finally, and perhaps most importantly, intern, intern, intern. Many schools have semester in DC programs – take advantage. Immersing yourself in the culture of politics is a great way to find out if it's the right path for you. Not spending a semester in DC is my second biggest undergrad regret (again, take economics!). Through a semester in DC or a summer program, you can take classes, intern part or full time, and meet other students from around the country who will become your future colleagues. It may be just what you need to land a permanent job at that organization or your dream job on Capitol Hill.

If a semester away isn't possible for financial or other reasons, you can still make the most of it at school. If you attend college in your state capital, the possibilities are endless. You can intern for a state representative, executive department, interest group, lobbyist, or political consulting firm. Most cities (big and otherwise) have local and state government offices, including state and local elected officials. There may be policy and interest groups, too, particularly if they focus on local issues. If you go to school in the boonies, you may need to adjust your class schedule to allow you to travel a day or two per week for an internship. You also may be able to create an independent study that allows you to get some hands-on experience in exchange for course credit. I worked out a plan that allowed me to do campus organizing around the elections during the fall semester and wrote a lengthy paper once the election was over.

Regardless of your circumstances, real world experience is infinitely more valuable than course work so get creative and figure out ways to gain the skills you'll need on the job. Make sure to spend enough time on your internship (10-20 hours per week) so that your supervisor gets to know you and can be an asset in your job hunt. Also, remember that a good attitude is everything when interning—more about that later.

Recent Grads (And Folks Who Never Went to College)

What's that you say? You majored in beer pong? Or college wasn't in the cards? No problem.

Yes, there are people who completed the Congressional Page program in high school, were stars on the debate team, and held nine internships while triple majoring in college (too close to home, Georgetown grads?). But, just because you didn't actively prepare for a career in politics doesn't mean you can't land a gig. You just have to work that much harder on the other pieces of the job puzzle.

If you're having trouble landing an interview, consider taking an unpaid internship. If your first reaction is, "Wait, did you say work for free?" then you had the right reaction, but you're probably going to have to do it anyway. DC is littered with young people looking for work who are more than happy to deliver coffee to other underpaid, overstressed congressional and nonprofit employees. Interning when you're out of school kind of stinks, but it's a great way in the door. It's OK to make your intentions clear and indicate that you would like a full-time position and are willing to do whatever it takes to make that happen. Work hard at every task, make yourself invaluable, and chances are they'll find the money to pay you somehow.

Finally, be open to every opportunity, even if it's not your dream job. At least it's a foot in the door in the industry of your choice. Remember, you're not going into politics to get rich—you're doing it because you want to make an impact. There are plenty of jobs on Wall Street if you're looking for more money working the same hours. If you're willing to be flexible (and possibly relocate), more unconventional jobs may come your way as well.

Career Switchers

Switching into politics later in life can be challenging. The most important thing is to manage your own expectations. You may see a political job as a lateral move, but chances are, you need to start a few rungs lower on the career ladder than you may think or hope. Talk to as many people as possible before you start applying for jobs. It is critical that you have a good sense of where you fit in and what roles are appropriate for someone with your background. Do your homework and research salaries so you have a realistic number in mind.

You also need a great, practiced, concise answer to "Why switch, why now?" If you're an out-of-work lawyer, employers may be worried that you'll go back to law once firms start hiring again. Sell your achievements as translatable skills: training, speaking, writing, teaching, leadership, and sales. For many career switchers, your experience can be a real selling point; you have a track record for judgment, problem-solving, and actual office issues. You likely have many relevant examples of how you handled situations. See Chapter 5 for more tips on discussing translatable skills on your resume and cover letters.

You should also get to know the jargon so you can write translatable skills bullets, and use appropriate language in interviews, not to mention while on the job. Jennie Blackton, now a prominent media consultant, started as a sitcom writer. She notes, "There's a steep learning curve as a career switcher, more than I had expected.

But, conversely, sometimes it can work for you. Don't be afraid to jump in and offer something new. Because you don't know the traditional routine, your unique perspective allows you, and those you work for, to get beyond the 'This is how things are always done' mantra."

Attend some political trainings (see Chapter 6 for some examples) so you can gain needed skills; you can usually attend trainings on weekends while at your current job. They are great networking opportunities, too.

At all points in the process, you should be answering the implied question, "Why you vs. someone else with more applicable experience?" Again, play up volunteer work, political trainings, and translatable skills. Your goal is to get the interview and convince them to go from maybe to yes by dazzling them in person. Be the "intriguing" candidate. Try to find someone to vouch for you, an established politico who can tell an employer that you have what it takes.

Many career switchers fall into one of the categories below.

Typical Career Switchers
⊃ **Lawyer to legislative staff**
You went to law school, maybe after a few years in political land. Then you landed a job at a big firm, and a few years in you hate it. You think, why not put that law degree to use actually writing the laws, right? Not always.

While this strategy may work in a state legislative office or on one of the committees, particularly if you have good in-state political contacts, the Hill is the Hill is the Hill and it's very tough to break in mid-career. You may see yourself as a legislative director but they see you as a legislative correspondent (who better to respond to constituent letters than a great writer who can analyze the bill?). However, you'll zoom up the career path faster than others once you take the lower-level job, given your past experience, maturity, and willingness to do whatever it takes to advance. If you have a particular area of expertise, say, patent law or international trade, you may be able to land as a legislative assistant to a legislator with relevant committee assignments. A few legislators, particularly those on the Judiciary Committee, do like to have lawyers on staff, but Hill experience is still key. Long story short, if you're willing to start over and take a serious (think 70%+) pay cut because you know this is what you want to do, put in a few years on the bottom of the totem pole and you'll soon find yourself in the job you craved all along.

⮑ Writer/Reporter/Blogger to press staff

You were a journalism major and spent a few years slugging it out on the metro desk at a small city newspaper. Then the recession hit, said newspaper folded, and you're out of a job. You used to cover city politics and government, so why not shape the story from the other side? In this scenario, you may in fact have a great in. You know how to write and what makes a strong pitch. You also know, for better or for worse, the other reporters on your beat. If you're familiar with a specific metro area or state, you may be able to land a job with a representative from that area. Your skills could also be put to use for a local campaign, labor union, association, interest group, or lobby shop in need of someone with strong communications skills. It's worth noting, though, that it may be difficult to go back to real journalism later, after being the mouthpiece for a politico.

If you were a writer or blogger in a different arena, say, food or entertainment, you need to develop some credentials within the political world. Start writing for political blogs, submitting stories to online magazines and journals, and pen thoughtful replies to prominent blog posts or online stories. If you don't have on-the-record experience, try to get some — volunteer for a small organization or serve as the press contact for a big charity event you're helping to plan. Again, you may need to start a little lower on the food chain than you would like, but you'll likely move up fast.

One caution to bloggers or editorial journalists: anything you say can and will be used against you in the court of public opinion. Expect the press secretary or communications director to read every one of your articles. If you slammed the party chairman two years ago in a late Friday night rant, it may be a deal killer (or asset, depending ...). Just be prepared to answer questions. Everything is fair game.

⊃ Business to nonprofit or campaign

If you're coming from the corporate sector, you probably have business acumen, see the inefficiencies of a nonprofit or government office, and want to solve everything right away. But some organizations aren't run like businesses.

The political work structure will probably be very shocking at first. In your past role, you may have had established processes, formal HR departments and a decent work-life balance. Welcome to your new life where someone 20 years your junior is your boss and you often sleep on a supporter's couch. Long-term planning might mean two weeks (or two days!), and almost no one is concerned with metrics like return on investment and net profit value. Emails from colleagues might be jarringly informal and the lingo is more confusing than your last CPA exam. Also, expect to spend nights and weekends talking about work incessantly; water cooler talk on Mondays revolves around your command of the Sunday talk shows.

It can be a tough transition – mainly because the skills you gained in the corporate sector may not be as widely accepted and acknowledged as they were in the past. Just remember that you don't know everything. Be humble when applying your skills to an entirely new scenario that includes tight budgets (dependent on a few wealthy donors or foundation funding), small staffs who wear many hats, and volunteers who are given tremendous responsibility with little accountability.

But you do have unique skills to improve some of the inefficiencies. The 80/20 rule that your boss trained you in? Highly relevant. Very basic modeling skills? You're likely the only person in the office who knows the intricacies of Excel. Project management expertise? You'll be a hero if you can strip down those processes into easy to implement rules for the office. Customer service best practices? A rarity anywhere in politics.

You'll have to do more menial labor, but you'll also advance much faster than you ever could have in the corporate world. In a year's time, an assistant can become a director. So, be prepared to ditch the suit and take out the trash.

➲ Volunteer campaigner to paid staffer

You've been your local precinct campaign or county committeeperson for a decade. You've circulated petitions to get candidates on the ballot and attended every pancake breakfast and rubber chicken dinner for city council up to U.S. Senate. For you, Columbus Day has real meaning; it's a day when you hand out candy emblazoned with candidate's faces and burn blisters into the soles of your feet walking alongside a Chevy Corvette carrying the local judge. You know everyone and everyone knows you, so hiring you as campaign staff is a no-brainer, right? Maybe.

A local or state campaign may be dying to have you handle their political outreach, so long as your reputation is that of a personable, hard-worker who gets things done. A more professionally run campaign for higher office will likely need more concrete skills. If you want to be an organizer, learn voter contact databases like Voter Activation Network (VAN) or Voter Vault, which you'll be asked to use on a daily, if not hourly, basis. There are trainings available to help you get up to speed. If you're looking to help with fundraising, make sure your resume reflects the work you've done raising money for candidates in the past, getting hard commitments, and raising to or exceeding your goal.

Also be aware of the hierarchy; just because you've known the candidate since she was in diapers doesn't mean you bypass the chain of command to make things happen.

The Political Ladder:
- ✓ Take Economics
- ✓ Make your mark through school or extracurriculars
- ✓ Get some real world experience
- ✓ Set realistic expectations for salary and title, particularly for career switchers
- ✓ Go on lots of informational interviews

EXECUTIVE ASSISTANT TO EXECUTIVE OFFICE: TYPES OF POLITICAL JOBS

A bit like the famous pregnancy book, *What to Expect When You're Expecting*, this chapter is a primer of what various campaign and political jobs are like. Think about trade-offs and what you want and need in a job.

The chart below demonstrates money vs. stability in the most common types of political jobs.

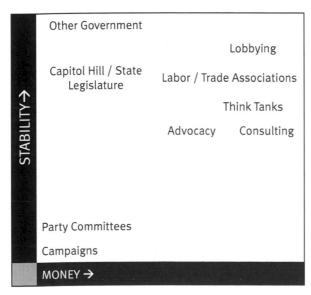

This chart checks-off various attributes (in my opinion) for common political jobs.

	Money	Stability	Impact	Fun
Campaigns			X	X
Party Committees			X	X
Capitol Hill / State Leg		X	X	
Other Government		X		
Advocacy			X	X
Lobbying	X	X	X	
Think Tanks	X	X		
Labor / Trade Associations		X	X	
Consulting	X		X	

I also recommend Joan Axelrod-Contrada's book, Career Opportunities in Politics, Government, and Activism, for detailed descriptions of political roles.

Campaigns

A campaign job means you're working for a candidate or issue campaign with a finite end, most often, Election Day. Usually this means you're working for a local, state or federal campaign, but ballot initiatives (or measures) also go in this category, as the feel of the campaign is similar.

If you're just starting out, think about your skill set. Are you great at talking to people? You would probably be a good field organizer. Super organized? Think about working as a scheduler. Persuasive and a good writer? Press Secretary. Uninhibited and persistent? Fundraising may be for you. Consultant Addisu Demissie notes, "If you work in politics, you start out in field or as an assistant. You have to earn your stripes."

Being a newbie can be an advantage though. "I actually like hiring campaign staff with less experience, because I can mold them and teach them how to be a good organizer," says Emmy Ruiz, an Obama campaign staffer.

Here is a brief overview of some of the most common types of campaign jobs:

Field Organizer – Most entry-level campaign staffers start out as field staff. Field just means talking to voters. You'll likely spend most of your day phone banking or canvassing voters in your district to either gauge their support, persuade them to support your candidate, or remind them to vote. You may also organize teams of volunteers to cover these tasks. All of this information is (hopefully) put into a database, such as the VAN or Voter Vault so the campaign can track their interest and voting behavior over time. Field is the heart of a campaign. Many organizations train future staff and volunteers on the do's and don'ts of field.

Field Director and Regional Field Organizer – More senior field jobs that supervise specific geographic areas or the entire district of the campaign. Responsible for managing field organizers and setting vote goals.

Advance Team – Sent to set up an event ahead of time by managing all details from sound to where the press corps will stay. Advance is another great entry-level job, usually only found on presidential and sometimes statewide campaigns.

Political Director – Often responsible for working with elected officials, constituency groups and allied organizations. This person works closely with the field team to make sure key voting constituencies and their leaders are an integral part of the campaign.

Policy Director – Not every campaign has one and this role may be combined with others. Most people entering campaigns think they want to be the policy director. Few people will actually do that job; fewer still will actually like doing it. This person is usually responsible for creating the campaign's views and messages around key issues, in close consultation with the candidate, campaign manager, and press team. Policy staff members are often experts in one or more issue areas and may also be responsible for responding to questionnaires or surveys from issue-focused organizations and the media.

Communications Director – Head of the press team and overseer of the campaign's messaging and relations with the press. This person may be the only communications staffer (and also take on the job responsibilities of the press secretary) or have a supporting team.

Press Secretary – Responsible for dealing with members of the press, including speaking on the record for the campaign, drafting and issuing press releases, pitching stories, staffing the candidate at press events, setting up editorial board interviews, and more. Press secretaries may also serve as the candidate's speechwriter. Press staff should be good writers and public speakers.

Research Director – Conducts research on the candidate, his or her opponent(s), and key issues. This job can be combined with press responsibilities or handled by a consultant on smaller campaigns. Excellent research skills and discretion are required, as this person may uncover information about his or her own candidate that the campaign does not want out in the open.

Online Team – These days, the online team can cross into many areas: field, fundraising, press. Roles may include webmaster, social media manager, grassroots fundraiser, and more. Due to the changing nature of technology, these roles are often carved out by each specific campaign and change rapidly. In addition, nearly every major campaign has a data manager with specialized training. If numbers are your thing, learn voter databases well and any campaign will be dying to have you.

Finance Director – Nothing on a campaign happens without money and this person is responsible for raising the cash. Responsibilities include writing and executing the finance plan, researching prospective donors, managing call time, overseeing fundraising events, reaching out to Political Action Committees (PAC) and allied interests, and compliance with relevant laws. "You need to be charismatic, organized, a strong writer, and comfortable being on the phone all day," says fundraising consultant Mike Berkowitz. "It's far from glamorous." Fundraising is a very valuable and transferable skill; often finance staffers are hired even before the campaign manager.

Finance Assistant – Finance directors will often have a deputy or assistant to help them with the massive task of raising money for the campaign. The finance assistant may manage call time with the candidate, conduct prospect research, enter relevant data and information into databases like NGP, or manage all of the events.

Compliance – Compliance means complying with the law, particularly around campaign finance. This may be handled by an outside consultant or vendor, but on larger-budget campaigns, there is usually one or more in-house staff that works with consultants or vendors.

Scheduler – This person is responsible for scheduling the candidate's time. He or she works closely with the candidate and campaign manager to respond to requests for appearances, schedule call time and fundraising events, and carve out personal and family time. Schedulers should be well organized, patient, and personable.

Campaign Manager –The campaign manager is a seasoned, experienced political professional who has likely served in another senior role on multiple campaigns. This person works closely with the candidate, staff, and any consultants to craft the day-to-day operations of a campaign as well as its overall direction.

Campaign Chairperson and Treasurer – These are part-time positions, usually unpaid, often friends of the candidate or important politicos.

Depending on the size and budget of the campaign, other roles may include press assistant, call time manager, deputy campaign manager, assistant to the candidate, volunteer coordinator, phone bank captain, opposition research director, tracker—and on and on!

Capitol Hill and State Legislative Staff

Whether you're working for a member of the U.S. Congress or your state legislature, the roles are often the same. First and foremost, you are responsible to your constituents. The citizens of your district or state elected your representative and the taxpayers pay your salary. They are your ultimate boss. Never lose sight of this fact, and you will always do your job well.

Second, these jobs, particularly on Capitol Hill, are very difficult to secure. Tom Manatos, who founded a famous jobs listserv and website, notes that Hill offices typically get 300-400 resumes *in the first 24 hours* after listing an entry-level job. Capitol Hill is its own beast – you can't easily make a lateral move from a state legislative office to another related field. Hill culture demands you work your way up. If you have your heart set on a Hill job, there are two tried and trusted ways in – start as an intern or staff assistant and work your way up or work on the campaign of a challenger or open-seat race and hope to win. Occasionally, people enter senior staff roles after years of lobbying or other work, but those opportunities are rare. CR Wooters, a former Chief of Staff, notes, "Most folks on the Hill work their way up the food chain. That is what I recommend for people who want to work directly with legislation. You need to understand how the Legislative Correspondent works before you can be an Legislative Assistant and you need to be an LA for a while before you can be the Legislative Director." More on that to follow.

It's easiest to get a job with the member from your home district or state, where you go to school, or where you currently live; use any connection possible to get in the door. If there aren't any current openings in the office, ask for an informational interview with the chief of staff. He or she can give you the lay of the land and you can ask to be notified of any future openings.

You should also think about the type of member you want to work for. Like politicos, they generally fall into two categories: hacks and wonks. Hacks are likely most concerned with the politics of the day and may be eyeing a leadership position or higher office. Wonks are policy-driven and want to make an impact on key issue areas. No matter what, every member is focused on re-election. What was your member's margin of victory last time? Are they a perennial target or a safe seat? These circumstances will help determine internal office politics and the type of staffer the office tries to hire.

Here is a brief overview of some of the most common types of Capitol Hill and legislative jobs:

Chief of Staff – Similar to a campaign manager, this person is responsible for day-to-day operations and the "big picture" workings of the DC or state capitol office as well as district offices. Often a seasoned operative, this person usually has worked his or her way up the ladder or served as campaign manager for a first-term representative.

Press Secretary – Responsible for dealing with members of the press, the press secretary speaks on the record for the member, drafts and issues press releases, pitches stories, staffs the member at press events, sets up editorial board interviews, and more. He or she may also serve as the member's speechwriter.

Scheduler – This person is responsible for scheduling the representative's time. They work closely with the member and chief of staff to schedule committee hearings, district events, personal time, and other events.

Legislative Staff – The number of state legislative staff will vary depending on whether they are a full-time or part-time legislature. Staff sizes will also vary in Congress, with freshman members having smaller budgets than more senior members and minority party members having fewer staff allocations than the majority party members. Staff ranges from legislative directors, who oversee strategy and staff, often with expertise in one or more issue areas; to legislative assistants, who are responsible for various issue areas or committee assignments; to legislative correspondents, who reply to constituent mail and inquiries. Generally, legislative staff start out with less weighty issues (like animal rights or funding for the arts) and then work their way up to issues of more responsibility (such as foreign affairs or appropriations) or work on the member's primary committee assignment. It helps to be a good writer with strong research skills.

Staff Assistant – This is an entry-level job responsible for general administrative duties and keeping the office working smoothly.

Intern – The single best way to secure a job on Capitol Hill is to intern while in college or as a recent graduate. No, you won't get paid but you will make invaluable contacts. Previous Hill experience is usually a pre-requisite for working on the Hill and the only way to get it is to intern.

District Office Staff – From district director on down to staff assistant (my first paid job in politics), the district staff is responsible for handling constituent problems and inquiries and maintaining strong ties to voters, key influencers, local elected officials, and the media.

Committee Staff – Each member is assigned to one or more committees, which focus on specific issue areas such as Agriculture or Defense, as well as Rules, Ways and Means, and Appropriations. Each committee has designated staff from both parties, usually former staff for members on the committee or issue experts on the policy areas under that committee's jurisdiction. Securing a committee job is even more difficult than getting a position in a member's office, but they do have entry-level positions.

Leadership Staff – And even more difficult than securing a committee job is working for leadership. These high-ranking members such as the Speaker of the House and Minority Whip receive appropriations for staff to oversee their leadership duties. These staff members are typically long-time employees of the member or senior staff from other member's offices as well as experts in parliamentary procedure. They work with members of their party, party committees, and (particularly if they are the party in power) the White House to pursue policy agendas and manage internal and external politics.

Nonprofits and Advocacy Organizations

The term "nonprofits" is a catchall for all types of organizations. According to the National Center for Charitable Statistics, there are over 1.5 million nonprofits in the United States. Maybe you want to work for a women's shelter or an international development organization, or you want to work for a national environmental group or your local food bank.

Most nonprofits have only a tangential relationship with what I categorize as politics. Some may do a little lobbying or have a

PAC that gives to local and state candidates. But most nonprofit organizations focus on their mission at hand and try to make the world (or at least their corner of it) a better place. There is much to be said for working at a nonprofit—you generally interact more with the people you're trying to help and see direct results of your work more quickly. They often have small staffs where you can have more responsibility earlier on and move up the ladder more quickly. Small budgets mean you'll never make a lot of money and other amenities may be few and far between, but you can sleep at night knowing you made a difference.

Then there are the monster nonprofits; for terms of discussion here, I'll refer to them as advocacy organizations. These are the Sierra Club's and National Rifle Associations of the world – organizations that depend on political action from their members and staff for survival and to further their mission and goals. These organizations often have multi-million dollar budgets with dozens of staff members who work on state and federal policy and politics, and state and local affiliates that assist with this work. They probably do non-partisan voter education work through their 501c3, have a PAC for political endorsements and donations, a 501c4 for voter persuasion work, and may also run independent expenditures. Whew!

If there is a specific issue you are passionate about, nothing may be as personally fulfilling as a career with an advocacy organization. There is no better way to learn the ins and outs of particular issues and the players involved in coalition politics for legislative and political battles. The hours are often more predictable, the pay and benefits a little better, and the job security more stable. Working for a state or local affiliate is a great way to be politically active without moving to DC or your state's capital, too. You can find additional information on advocacy organizations on opensecrets.org.

Big nonprofits are a lot like corporations – rigid on titles, salary, benefits, and promotions. The bureaucracy and slower pace may be a negative to some. Again, consider your needs and wants before diving in, but you can never go wrong with a few years of advocacy experience under your belt.

One thing to note: on campuses and in major cities, you may see job flyers or ads that say things like "Work for the Environment!" Know what you're getting into – these jobs are mainly about fundraising, not advocacy. You will spend your time going door to door or standing on a street corner asking people for low-dollar donations. But these positions can be great entry-level or part-time jobs, and you gain valuable experience as a canvasser or canvass manager, which can be put to use in a campaign setting.

Labor Unions and Trade Associations

Labor and trade associations can be terrific places to work if you want something more stable or are interested in a particular industry. Working for organized labor can be a great move for progressive politicos and shouldn't be ruled out by Republicans (unless you fundamentally disagree with their agenda). Unions represent thousands or millions of workers in a particular industry or industries. The National Education Association represents 3.2 million teachers while the International Union of Elevator Constructors represents 25,000 members. On the other side of labor unions are trade associations, which represent the business side of an industry.

Large, politically active labor unions and trade associations will often run multiple political programs during key elections. Whether you work on member-to-member programs or independent expenditures, these programs operate like campaigns, with phone bank and canvass programs, direct mail, and paid media. Labor unions and trade associations are great places to cut your teeth in politics, with some additional stability not provided by electoral campaigns. They often have large political and legislative departments that help further policy goals by educating members on key issues and mobilizing them for elections and grassroots lobbying. Unions also have departments that work on member benefits, pensions, collective bargaining, and other key areas.

No matter the size, labor unions and trade associations are powerful forces in local, state, and national politics. In many respects, the pluses and minuses of unions and associations are similar to advocacy organizations. And, like advocacy organizations, they often have state and local infrastructure that allows staff to work from a variety of locations.

Think Tanks

Wonks, this is your section. You need the ability to think, research, analyze, write (not just well, but succinctly and fast), and argue both sides of an issue. At their core, think tanks are the epicenter of long-term policy development. Neera Tanden, President of the Center for American Progress, says, "Think tanks are the ideas infrastructure; they have the luxury of time to think things through and look at solutions for what's coming over the horizon."

Any kind of advanced degree is an asset here. You may work for an academic, policy expert, or ex-politician; you'll likely be encouraged to create and publish your own research. As a prominent conservative think tank staffer notes, "You have to be able to research, write, and sell your ideas. It's not just an intellectual exercise; for your ideas to be implemented, you need excellent communication and persuasion skills."

Partisan, bi-partisan, non-partisan, there's a think tank (or a policy institute) out there that fits your political ideology and focuses on the issues you care about. Examples of political think tanks include: Aspen Institute, Brookings Institute, Cato Institute, Center for American Progress, Council on Foreign Relations, and Heritage Foundation. Harvard's Kennedy School of Government has an exhaustive list: http://www.hks.harvard.edu/library/research/guides/think-tanks-directory.htm.

Lobbying and Public Relations

Contrary to popular belief, lobbyist is not an evil word. In fact, in the lobbying world, contacts and reputation are everything, so lobbyists are careful not to lie or scheme when dealing with clients.

You name the group, cause, or belief and they have a lobbyist – or 12. Lobbyists are often former Hill and legislative staffers with expertise in a particular issue. They usually have strong relationships with elected officials and their staff. Yes, they represent "special interests" and sometimes those special interests are corporations. But they often provide important, detailed information on technical legislative issues and help make an issue real by bringing in constituents. Lobbyists are paid to provide unfiltered expertise on an issue and to make that issue position heard in legislative offices and executive agencies. "Most of what I do is educate," says Julie Philp, a Republican lobbyist for the National Association of Chain Drug Stores. "Our members are constituents and not everyone can come to DC to speak to their member of Congress. So I advocate on their behalf."

If you work for a lobby shop, you may not need to be a registered federal lobbyist. There are plenty of other roles that lobby firms play, with actual lobbying being just one tool in the arsenal.

As a grassroots lobbyist, you'll likely work with diverse coalitions to develop political and legislative strategies at the state and federal level. You might help contact local constituents about an issue or encourage them to contact their member. Or maybe you'll craft media strategies in member's districts to call attention to your client's issue. All of these are valuable, transferable skill sets that will serve you well in other jobs.

Lobbyists serve an important function and becoming a lobbyist can be a lucrative career move after many years on the Hill or with an advocacy organization.

Consulting Firms

This category encompasses a wide swath of businesses that do political work and often take on corporate and nonprofit clients as well. The number of political consultants has exploded in recent years. Consulting firms are usually founded and staffed by seasoned professionals, along with some entry-level and mid-level employees. These pros have amassed long careers in politics and have strong relationships with elected officials, labor unions, trade associations, and advocacy organizations. Media consultant J.J. Balaban notes, "Being a consultant is fundamentally different than being a campaign staffer. But the most important requirement of any consultant is an ample amount of experience working as a staffer on campaigns. The worst consultants are the ones who don't have a strong understanding of what it's like working on the ground every day." Campaign veteran Adam Weiss' first job out of college was with a direct mail firm. His boss told him, "You won't be doing anything strategic, political or creative, but if you keep your eyes and ears open, you might learn something."

Consulting firms may pay more and allow you the opportunity to work for a variety of clients, but many consulting shops staff like campaigns and hire mostly seasonal staff—i.e., you're out of a job come Thanksgiving. You should expect long hours, particularly during election season. Consulting firms are a great way to get experience with a little more stability.

However, as a friend explained, "Consultants care about getting paid, winning, and their influence, in that order." There's not really a penalty for losing, so watch out for you. And assume consultants have more influence than you think—they may actually be running the campaign.

Here are some examples of consultants:

General Consultants – Like a campaign manager, general consultants are often involved in all aspects of the campaign and related decision-making. They also help coordinate other consultants such as pollsters, media, and direct mail, or they may fill one of these roles themselves.

Direct Mail – Around election time, pamphlets magically appear in voters' mailboxes encouraging them to vote for candidate X or ballot initiative Y. Those mailings are the result of months of targeting, polling, research, writing, and design all coordinated by direct mail firms. They work closely with campaigns, labor unions, trade associations, and advocacy organizations to find voters who will be influenced by a carefully honed message brought to life with graphics and photos. Many direct mail firms also act as general consultants and some are branching out into online ads as well.

Pollsters – Polling is both science and art. Pollsters craft questions to survey the opinions of voters and analyze the results. They work closely with media teams and other consultants to craft a candidate's message. A background in statistics or quantitative analysis is usually required to advance in the polling field.

Media consultants – Media firms create TV, radio, and online ads for campaigns and often take on corporate and interest group clients as well. While most firms specialize in media buying (literally buying the time needed for the ads to run) or the creative side of creating the ads, many cover the entire process.

Fundraising Consultants – Often, fundraising consultants are hired to raise money from PACs and interest groups in DC. They may also oversee the general fundraising strategy for a campaign.

Party Committees

Both sides of the aisle have national committees that focus on presidential and party politics like the Democratic National Committee and Republican National Committee as well as committees that focus on congressional, Senate, Gubernatorial, and state legislative races. These committees provide support to elected officials and candidates, fundraise for the party, research and provide broad messaging, and oversee the official party processes such as nominations and conventions.

Working for state and national party committees can be a great entre in or an excellent next career step after several cycles on campaigns. Committees are typically staffed by seasoned professionals as well as entry-level support staff. State and national party committees staff up like a campaign and typically keep a small staff for off-years.

Working for the Government (Non-Political)

Whether you want to work at the White House or for your county or municipal government, there are a few key things to keep in mind if you want to work for the government.

First, you work for the people. You may have loyalty to a particular party or elected official but your first loyalty is to your constituents. Government entities and departments are cash-strapped, bureaucratic, and sometimes inefficient. It's your job to work hard and stretch tax payer dollars while serving the public interest. You're playing an important role that impacts people's daily life. Constituents depend on you to get their trash picked up, their Social Security check, and more. Whether you're an assistant in the West Wing or an assistant in your city councilman's office, the work you do matters.

Relationships also matter. It's important to be qualified for a job, but working your networks helps in landing a government job. Get to know local elected officials and staff through official means like town hall meetings as well as political events. Working on a local campaign, even as a volunteer, may help you land a permanent job. Being a community activist on a key issue may get you an appointment to a commission. Hiring practices are, and should be, non-political, but relationships may help you get the interview.

Third, no politics on the job. You cannot use your work computer or phone for political purposes, you cannot conduct political work during business hours, and you need to make sure it's OK for you to do anything political during your off hours. In fact, most federal employees are prohibited from these activities under the Hatch Act. Again, you work for the people and their tax dollars pay your salary. If it feels wrong, it probably is. When in doubt, ask.

If you work on a winning campaign, there is no guarantee that you will secure a job in the government. The higher the office, the more this statement rings true. If you are a field organizer on a presidential campaign, it may take a year or more for your government job to come through—first come Senate confirmations for Cabinet officials and senior staff, then mid-level staff hirings, then low-level staff—all coupled with background checks, of course.

About those background checks: never, ever lie. Being busted for having some pot on you at a party in college isn't an immediate disqualification for the job, but lying about it sure is. Also think carefully about your references and be prepared to provide a list of every employer and supervisor you ever had as well as every landlord.

Depending on what job you are searching for, USAjobs.gov allows you to search for federal positions around the country and by department, keyword, and salary level.

USE YOUR ASSETS: YOUR RESUME

Your resume is the single most important tool you have in your job search. In fact, it may be the only way people hear or learn about you. So it better be good.

My friend Gayle Laakmann McDowell, author of *The Google Resume* and founder of CareerCup.com, put it best, "Resumes should highlight what you did, not what you were supposed to do." When writing your resume, you should always be thinking about what makes you stand out from everyone else. You need quantifiable results and accomplishment-based bullets in a simple format.

While you should have a flawless, generic resume that you can send out on a moment's notice, ideally, you should tailor your resume for every position. It's helpful to have one long version with slightly varied bullets emphasizing different aspects of your skills in the same job, so you can just cut and paste as needed. Job descriptions are clue sheets! Read them carefully to see what type of candidate they're looking for and which skills are the key to success. If you're applying to a large company or organization, they may use a computer program to scan for keywords, so thesaurus up your resume (and cover letter) to match what they're saying. Mirror your skills to what the company wants while being honest about past experiences.

Also, update your resume while in your current position as you gain new responsibilities or complete projects. This will make it that much easier to create bullets that indicate accomplishments with specific metrics. And it's always a good idea to have an updated resume on hand for any unexpected opportunities.

Political resumes are a little different than other resumes. This is not a functional resume industry. If you're a career switcher, the resume I outline below may look and feel a lot different than what you're used to handing out.

Basic Content

I have three examples at the end of this chapter: entry-level, mid-level, and senior (both a one-pager and a two-pager). But here are the basics to include, listed from top to bottom.

Name: You want people to remember it, so make the font a little larger (12-20 point) so it stands out (bold, italics, or underline).

Contact information: Current address, phone number, and a professional email address (a variation of your name is best).

Objective: You only need an objective to express something that can't be said in another way. Usually they're only needed for career switchers and entry-level professionals (see Jill Jones' resume as an example). If you include one, be sure to tailor it to the specific job. Another version of an objective is a Qualifications Summary, which can be helpful for career switchers, recent college grads, and more senior professionals who have had a variety of jobs.

Work experience or political experience:
- If you primarily have politically-focused work experience, create one chronological list, with your most recent job first. If you mainly have volunteer political experience or just a few

internships under your belt, create a separate section like "Political Experience" to highlight what is most relevant (see Jill Jones' resume). List your most recent work first. Then you can create a section below outlining your other relevant work experience in chronological order.

- Always list your employer, title, location, and dates worked. If you're a more seasoned professional, title is probably more important than employer, so feel free to list it first or bold the title. If you held multiple titles on the same campaign or for the same organization, list the most recent one first and then indicate your promotion in your bullets (see Jamie Ryan's resume). If you worked in multiple states or locations throughout a campaign, abbreviate in order to keep the info on one line and highlight any regional work in your bullets.
- Bullets should be concise. No first person and no pronouns!
- Don't just reiterate your job description. Nikki Enfield, former executive director of Democratic GAIN, says, "I speak politics. I know what a field organizer or a legislative assistant does on a day-to-day basis. What makes you better than all the others who also did your job?" You can ask your former boss or co-workers to help you brainstorm. What did you focus on? Maybe include one bullet for each major area of work; see my resume for a good example. If you're having trouble creating concise bullets, you're probably re-stating your job description rather than focusing on what you did well.
- Quantify, quantify, quantify. Use numeric examples like "increased turnout by 7%" or "Recruited 73 volunteers for GOTV shifts." (See Jamie Ryan's resume.)
- Use action verbs like wrote, managed, directed, and led. You can find many more examples by Googling "action verbs resumes."

What are your translatable skills?

Maybe you haven't worked in politics for very long but you were a sales rep or a paralegal. Chances are you picked up a few skills along the way.

The summer between my junior and senior years of college, I worked as a sales associate at the Gap. Not terribly political, right? But I had a direct supervisor I had to report to and co-workers I dealt with every day. I had daily and weekly goals and had to learn a new computer system (i.e., the cash register). I interacted with customers to answer questions and solve problems. This sounds a lot like a field position, right?

A friend who was a manager at McDonald's while working his way through college said he learned more about politics through that job than on any campaign.

Look for ways to describe your non-political work in political terms.

Education: Keep this short and sweet. Again, we don't care if you went to Harvard. In most instances, the name of your school, location, major, and graduation year are all that's needed. If you're a wonk and applying for policy jobs, list a few relevant courses or the title of your thesis. List your GPA only if it's above 3.5 or if you graduated with honors.

Skills: If you're fluent in Spanish or speak conversational Arabic, list it here. Familiar with voter contact databases or web tools? This is where you brag. If you've gone through the EMILY's List fundraiser's training or Wellstone Action!'s campaign manager school, list the dates you attended and a brief bullet. Blogging is not a skill (unless you're applying for a social media job). Microsoft Office is also not a skill; it's a requirement. Anything the average person can do should not be listed in the skills section. (See Jill Jones' resume for good examples.)

Awards: It's OK to list awards if they are prominent or significant, demonstrate a skill, or if you can quantify to add value (chosen out of over 300 applicants, for example).

Webpages: If you have significant web experience or are applying for a web-based or social media job, include a link to a representative example. Some people also list their LinkedIn or About.Me pages; this is only helpful if there is significant information on these sites you could not articulate through your resume. Otherwise, it's just kind of cheesy.

Hobbies and Interests: We don't care about your personal interests. Don't take up valuable space listing hobbies on your resume unless you're into something unique and can use it as a conversation starter in an interview.

Resume Tips 101:

- Keep it to one page! If you have less than 10 years' experience in professional politics (as in, paid jobs), your resume should not be more than one page. A one page resume forces you to pick the best, most relevant work and accomplishments. If you have more than 10 years' experience, it's OK to go to two pages, but you should still keep bullets succinct. Look at the one-page and two-page versions of my resume; I have never felt the need to use the two-pager. I throw away two-page resumes from recent college grads.
- To save even more space, cut your college experience down, shorten your sentences, take out your objective, put all contact info on one line, or drop a .5 point in font size.
- Grammar pet peeves: The D in Democrat and R in Republican are always capitalized. Quotation marks go after the period.

Numbers one through nine are spelled out; 10 and above are numeric.

- Keep it easy to read. Font style and size go together; 11-point Arial may take up the same room as 12-point Calibri. Play around with what size and styles you like best, but never go below 10 point font and stay away from fancy styles. You should have at least a half inch margin on all sides. Take advantage of bold, underline, italics, indents, and bullets – they help make key information stand out and keep everything organized. Be consistent throughout with the format. (Do you have periods at the end of each bullet? The same type of bullet?)
- You will lose formatting if you have to cut and paste your resume into a text box online so have a version on hand that only utilizes capitalization for emphasis.
- Be thorough and truthful. It's fine to have gaps in employment or to tend bar for a while to pay the bills – we all do it. Better a good non-political job than a bad political job. Don't exaggerate how long you were with an employer or embellish your title or responsibilities. Politics is a small world and your employer or references will find out!

Remember to proofread your resume. Any mistake could be an immediate disqualification. Don't just rely on spell check – it can confuse similar words and change your meaning. Nothing is more valuable than an experienced set of eyes looking your resume over and giving personal feedback. I recommend having a fellow politico review it to make sure your bullets make sense and then have a non-political friend look it over to flag any political speak that wouldn't make sense to the average person (or average human resources staffer).

And never cover up who you are. I once had a college student ask me if it was OK to be "out" on his resume. In a word, yes—if it's relevant to your experience. If you were treasurer of the campus

LGBTQ organization, list it. You don't want to work for anyone who is uncomfortable with any part of your identity.

The Political Ladder:
- ✓ Create a perfect, triple spell-checked generic resume
- ✓ Call former bosses and co-workers as needed to help you craft accomplishment-driven bullets for your resume
- ✓ Have a non-political as well as a political friend triple-check your resume

Entry-level resume

JILL JONES

222 Miller Rd • Washington, DC 12345 •

(202) 555-9876 • jilljones@gmail.com

OBJECTIVE

To obtain an entry-level position on a Democratic political campaign where I can learn and expand my skill set while working towards victory.

POLITICAL EXPERIENCE

OSU College Democrats   *Columbus, OH*
Vice-President   4/10 – Present
Publicity Committee Chair   4/09 – 4/10
- Manage club with over 700 members; work directly with five committee chairs to further organizational goals around membership, press/public relations, technology, campaigns, and fundraising
- Helped organize campus campaign for 2010 elections, including recruiting over 400 GOTV volunteers for over 1,100 shifts
- Serve as organizational representative to Student Association
- Member of Ohio Democratic Party Steering Committee

Ohio Democratic Party   *Washington, DC*
Intern   6/11 – 8/11
- Provided support for Press Department including eight staff and department head
- Created new media database with over 300 websites, blogs, Facebook pages, and other Twitter feeds
- Drafted over two dozen press releases on key issues
- Advanced press events for state party chairman and local and state candidates

OTHER WORK EXPERIENCE

Nanny   2007 – Present
- Provided in-home child care for ages ranging from newborn to 12
- Consistently worked for same family for over four years
- Provided homework help and cooked family meals on occasion

Camp Whispering Pine   *Green Springs, OH*
Counselor   Summer 2008 & 2009
- Supervised one dozen 15-year-olds for eight weeks at sleep-away camp
- Managed day to day activities and directed camp play, "Charlie Brown"

EDUCATION

Ohio State University   *Columbus, OH*
B.A. in Political Science   Expected May 2012
- Member of Gay-Straight Alliance and Women's Center in addition to OSU Democrats

SKILLS

HTML, Voter Activation Network (VAN), VoteBuilder
Campus Camp Wellstone Training   March 2010

Mid-level resume

JAMIE RYAN

1065 Pennsylvania Street, Apt. 308 Washington, DC 20003 JRyan23@gmail.com (202) 555-9876

PROFESSIONAL EXPERIENCE

Organizing for America
Canada Field Director July 2010 to Present

- Manage four field staff that recruit, train, and empower volunteer organizers to support the President's message
- Write and implement field plan at the statewide level; analyzed and adapted field metrics on a daily basis
- Develop training programs for staff and volunteers; provide motivation and direction to our volunteer base at events and statewide conference calls; manage over 3,200 statewide volunteers
- Managed a staff of over thirty regional field directors and organizers during the mid-term election to get-the-vote-out for Senator Orlando

Northern Ontario Regional Field Director October 2009 to July 2010

- Worked in Ontario's 1st and 2nd Congressional District to support President Obama's agenda at the grassroots level
- Identified and developed local community organizers through tailored training programs, developed outreach plans to strengthen our organizational structure and reach voter contact goals
- Successfully lobbied Congresswoman O'Brian to support of health insurance reform on both key votes in the House of Representatives

Barack Obama's Campaign for Change
Bloomington, ON Field Organizer August to November 2008

- Organized a voter contact program in Bloomington, Ontario, recruiting and training hundreds of volunteers that registered new voters, delivered Senator Obama's message, and encouraged more supporters to vote early and get to the polls on Election Day
- Historically red county voted in favor of Barack Obama, 54% to 43%, and had over 95% voter turnout

Environment Ontario
Clean Energy Associate/Assistant Canvass Director January to August 2008

- Researched and wrote fact sheets given to state legislators on specific bills
- Organized press conferences, pitched stories to local reporters, responded to articles in recent press, and organized a "Solar Barbeque" for state lawmakers
- Built a coalition of 43 businesses and organizations around legislative platform
- Hired and trained a staff of 25 to raise money, build membership and do campaign work for Environment Ontario and the Ontario Public Interest Research Group

Congressman Mark John's Washington, DC Office
Intern July to August 2006

- Compiled a record of all of the Congressman's votes during the 109th Congress and created database to allow for easier replies to constituent inquiries
- Assisted with constituent services including responding to mail and email, organizing tours of the Capitol, and staffed Congressman

Senator Ken Salazar's Washington, DC Office
Intern May to July 2006

- Worked with the energy and environment staff to take part in the formulation and oversight of energy legislation

EDUCATION

University of Colorado at Boulder
Summa cum Laude, with a B.A. in Environmental Policy August 2003 to December 2007

Advanced resume (short)

ALEXANDRA ACKER-LYONS

987 Main Street • Mountain View, CA 94041 • 202-555-1234 • alexandra@gmail.com

PROFESSIONAL EXPERIENCE

Youth Engagement Fund — Mountain View, CA
Director — *September 2011-present*
- Manage dynamic investment of individual donors and civic engagement foundations to fund youth-focused groups and projects working on voter registration and get out the vote activities.

Share Our Strength — Mountain View, CA
Consultant, No Kid Hungry Campaign — *February 2011-present*
- Created new youth engagement program for national organization working to end childhood hunger.
- Manage online and offline program activities, including pilot program for five college-aged Youth Ambassadors.

Democratic GAIN — Washington, DC
Executive Director — *October 2009-December 2010*
- Managed national membership association for political professionals with over 47,000 members.
- Set annual goals and strategy with staff and Board of Directors comprised of leading political professionals.
- Led fundraising activities, including corporate giving, major institutional donors, and low-dollar events.
- Oversaw largest online political job board and resume database. Worked with thousands of job seekers and hundreds of organizations and companies to connect political talent to employers.

Training Director — *December 2004-August 2005*
- Managed all aspects of trainings for political professionals including writing curriculum, agendas, marketing materials, logistics, preparing outside trainers, and recruiting participants.

Young Democrats of America — Washington, DC
Executive Director — *March 2007-April 2009*
- Oversaw nation's largest youth-focused, political organization with over 2,300 chapters in all 50 states.
- Created first-ever strategic plan for organization and managed six national and eight state-based staff to successfully meet monthly and yearly benchmarks. Led 15-member Board of Directors to meet goals.
- Managed $1.5M annual budget and all fundraising activities. Liaised with major donors and oversaw low-dollar monthly giving program.
- Directed paid and volunteer campaign programs that contacted 200,000 voters in 2008.
- Recognized youth vote expert with regular appearances in national television, print, and radio outlets.

Lawyers' Committee for Civil Rights Under Law — Washington, DC
Campaign Manager, National Campaign for Fair Elections — *October 2005- March 2007*
- Managed national Election Protection program and federal and state election reform activities. Provided communications, grassroots organizing, and advocacy support to state coalitions working on voting rights issues.
- Organized Election Protection programs in 19 states with over 2,000 legal volunteers for the 2006 election.

John Kerry for President and the Democratic National Committee — Washington, DC
National Youth Outreach Director — *May 2004-November 2004*
- Created national network of youth activists and recruited over 50,000 online volunteers.
- Developed organizing materials, training manuals, talking points, and internet organizing tools.

Planned Parenthood Federation of America — Washington, DC
Campus Outreach Manager — *August 2003-May 2004*
- Directed grassroots organizing and legislative advocacy efforts for over 150 campus groups.
- Managed $250,000 program budget and wrote quarterly and year-end reports for grant funder.

Democratic Congressional Campaign Committee — Washington, DC
Assistant to the Chair, Congresswoman Nita M. Lowey — *May 2001-December 2002*

Office of Congresswoman Nita M. Lowey (D-NY) — White Plains, NY
Staff Assistant — *May 2000-May 2001*

EXTRACURRICULAR LEADERSHIP

National Democratic Institute, *Consultant, Kuwait and Morocco programs* — *April 2009; July 2010; January 2011*

EDUCATION

State University of New York at Binghamton. B.A. in Political Science, *magna cum laude.* — *May 2000*

Advanced resume (long)

ALEXANDRA ACKER-LYONS
987 Main Street ▪ Mountain View, CA 94041 ▪ 202-555-1234 ▪ alexandra@gmail.com

PROFESSIONAL EXPERIENCE

Youth Engagement Fund Mountain View, CA
Director *Sept 2011-present*
- Manage dynamic investment of individual donors and civic engagement foundations to fund youth-focused groups and projects working on voter registration and get out the vote activities.
- Work with over 40 youth organizations to create effective programs and collaborative projects.

Share Our Strength Washington, DC
Consultant, No Kid Hungry Campaign *Feb 2011-present*
- Created new youth engagement program for national organization working to end childhood hunger.
- Manage online and offline program activities, including pilot program for five college-aged Youth Ambassadors.

Democratic GAIN Washington, DC
Executive Director *Oct 2009-Dec 2010*
- Managed national membership association for political professionals with over 47,000 members.
- Set annual goals and strategy with Board of Directors comprised of leading political professionals. Managed staff, vendors, consultants, and Advisory Board to effectively execute plan.
- Led fundraising activities, including corporate giving, major institutional donors, and low-dollar events.
- Oversaw largest online political job board and resume database. Worked with thousands of job seekers and hundreds of organizations and companies to connect political talent to employers.

Training Director *Dec 2004-Aug 2005*

- Managed all aspects of trainings for political professionals including writing curriculum, agendas, marketing materials, logistics, preparing outside trainers, and recruiting participants.
- Led introductory and advanced trainings for political professionals including campus organizing, communications, field and GOTV, and fundraising.

Young Democrats of America Washington, DC
Executive Director *March 2007-April 2009*
- Oversaw nation's largest youth-focused, political organization with over 2,300 chapters in all 50 states.
- Created first-ever strategic plan for organization and managed six national and eight state-based staff to successfully meet monthly and yearly benchmarks. Led 15-member Board of Directors and 200 National Committee members to direct long-term organizational goals.
- Managed $1.5M annual budget and all fundraising activities. Liaised with major donors and oversaw low-dollar monthly giving program.
- Served as press spokesperson and created all media materials. Recognized youth vote expert with regular appearances in national television, print, and radio outlets.
- Directed paid and volunteer campaign programs that contacted 200,000 voters in 2008. Led activist trainings and issue advocacy to identify and turnout young voters, recruit new members, and grow chapter network.

Lawyers' Committee for Civil Rights Under Law Washington, DC
Campaign Manager, National Campaign for Fair Elections *Oct 2005- March 2007*
- Managed national Election Protection program and federal and state election reform activities, including prioritizing policy agenda, legislative advocacy, coalition-building, and volunteer recruitment.
- Organized Election Protection programs in 19 states with over 2,000 volunteers for the 2006 election.
- Coordinated state legislative strategy for the National Network for Election Reform, providing communications, grassroots organizing, and legislative analysis to state coalitions working on voting rights issues.
- Drafted numerous grant proposals for foundations and individual funders.
- Developed website, www.nationalcampaignforfairelections.org, to communicate with voters and decision makers about policy issues and election reform news and events. Recruited 12,000 online activists.

John Kerry for President and the Democratic National Committee　Washington, DC
National Youth Outreach Director　May 2004-Nov 2004
- Created national network of youth activists and recruited over 50,000 online volunteers.
- Developed organizing materials, training manuals, talking points, and internet organizing tools.
- Organized hundreds of surrogate events in battleground states.
- Developed youth-oriented materials including organizing and training manuals, talking points, campaign literature, and internet organizing tools.
- Organized hundreds of surrogate events in battleground states designed to generate media coverage, excite activists, and recruit new volunteers.
- Worked with national, state and local allies to develop activist base and create message events.

Planned Parenthood Federation of America　Washington, DC
Campus Outreach Manager　Aug 2003-May 2004
- Managed $250,000 program budget for national youth activities for Planned Parenthood's 124 state and local affiliates and over 150 Planned Parenthood student groups. Supervised Campus Outreach staff to implement program activities.
- Coordinated national, state and local campus activities including grassroots organizing activities, legislative advocacy efforts, and media events. Organized and led field and media trainings for campus chapter leaders and affiliate staff.
- Created extensive organizing guides for staff and students, press materials for national President, and produced quarterly newsletter.

Democratic Congressional Campaign Committee　Washington, DC
Assistant to the Chair, Congresswoman Nita M. Lowey　May 2001-Dec 2002
- Served as body person, coordinated all political scheduling, and assisted with fundraising activities for Congresswoman Lowey.
- Organized and staffed travel to targeted candidate districts.
- Attended race reviews and political briefings on behalf of Congresswoman Lowey.

Office of Congresswoman Nita M. Lowey (D-NY)　White Plains, NY
Staff Assistant　May 2000-May 2001
- Responsible for responding to constituent inquiries, organizing press packets, and office administration.
- Staffed the Congresswoman at district events.
- Organized district intern program; supervised more than 20 college and high school interns.

EXTRACURRICULAR LEADERSHIP

National Democratic Institute
Consultant, Kuwait and Morocco programs　April 2009; July 2010; Jan 2011

Wharton Partners Club
Co-President　Sept 2009-Oct 2010

EDUCATION

State University of New York at Binghamton
Bachelor of Arts in Political Science, *magna cum laude*.　May 2000

BEER AND BUSINESS CARDS: THE ART OF NETWORKING

Now that you've figured out your needs and wants and read up on types of political jobs, it's time to start your hunt.

How can you find your dream job? Or any job? I can pretty much guarantee it won't be handed to you; you have to use your networks. You need to search it out, be persistent, and use all available tools. "There's no magic to getting a job in politics, just a lot of luck and hard work," says Mag Gottlieb of The George Washington University's Graduate School of Political Management. "And sometimes you need to make your own luck."

Who Can Help You?

First, make a list of your relevant contacts. You can use the template here and a simple Microsoft Excel spreadsheet to do the trick. I've used this tool for several job hunts. When I moved to Philadelphia a few years back, I made a list of everyone I knew in Pennsylvania or who had worked in PA politics. I started off with about a dozen names. As I met with those folks or talked to them over the phone, they introduced me to additional contacts, and on and on. I tracked everything in my spreadsheet, being sure to note who introduced me to a new contact. At the end of my search, I had over 100 names and had met, talked to, or emailed with nearly all of them. Keep an open mind; my single most helpful contact was a friend of a friend and a Republican lobbyist to boot.

F Name	L Name	Organization	Email	Phone	Notes	Referred
Jose	Rodriguez	NCHI	jose@nchi.org	202-555-1234	ran city council race	Mary K
Sally	Pierce	Women for Afghanistan	spierce@bmail.com	321-555-6543	knows Jane from college	Jane
Mike	Ewing	O'Brien for Senate	mewing@obrien4senate.org	579-555-8642	FD last cycle for Thomas	me

Tom Manatos, a former Hill staffer and founder of tommanatos-jobs.com, calls this building your web. "What makes me, me? What is my background and who matches it? Who went to my high school, college, is of the same religion, or is from the same ethnic background? Draw a line from you to the people who have similar backgrounds that you want to meet; that personal connection will help you get connected."

Next, add to your list people who have your dream job and people who work a few rungs below them. For instance, if you want to be a chief of staff on Capitol Hill, try to meet with a staff assistant or legislative assistant. Try to figure out who gets things done, as it may not be the person with the fancy title but, in fact, the youngest person on staff. As political consultant Addisu Demissie put it, "People who are important often don't act like it, but people who aren't important act like they are." You should also add any known political connectors—the people who are always on the

Host Committee for political fundraisers or show up at every event. Connectors are critical—they make a habit of bringing people together and may even like the challenge of helping someone new. You can reach out to them and ask for an informational interview (more about that in Chapter 7).

It's also helpful to research the career paths of people ahead of you, particularly those in your dream job. Google them, go to company websites, and look them up on LinkedIn. Ask yourself: "How did this person get from Job A to Job B; what were they thinking?" This can give you a sense of good vs. bad entry level jobs, which organizations promote from within, and how long it may take you to achieve a certain level of success.

What is Networking?

Networking can sound like a fancy, shallow means to an end. But really you're just meeting new people, many of whom can and will be helpful to you now or in the future. This is networking: You're at a happy hour and actively go up to new people, introduce yourself, and talk to them rather than the two or three friends you already know. Break the ice—the first conversation is at an event, the second can be an informational interview.

A principle goal of elected officials is to connect people (constituents) with ideas to create solutions – so politics tends to reward those who network. It's about who you know as well as what you know, so you want to know as many people as possible.

Good grades, a good resume, and a good cover letter isn't enough. Even good experience isn't enough. You need a personal network of people who can help you. But you can't create a network out of thin air when looking for a job.

Networking is the key to your job hunt; everyone is a potential connector or contact. Working in a transient sector like politics means you may have more jobs over shorter periods of time than your friends in other fields; I had eight jobs over 10 years in politics. But it allows you to meet more people and therefore expand your network. Politics is a small world and personal connections can make all the difference.

Don't forget about your friends and peers, and reach out to them as well as your former boss. Eli Center, a former campaign and consulting professional, says, "Resumes and cover letters don't get you jobs—friends do."

You will be amazed at how willing people are to help you with your job hunt. This is particularly true for politicos who have experienced what you're going through first-hand. People genuinely like helping others, but it's also nice to have an IOU. Be wary though; not everyone is your friend and these relationships can become transactional very fast. "Always watch out for those who are quick to use others for personal gains," says Hill and campaign veteran Jasper Hendricks. "Develop thick skin if you don't have one already."

Be nice to everyone. Not only is it the right thing to do, but you never know who or where someone will be in five years. Thank the assistant who brought you water before the interview and remember his or her name.

Companies and organizations get plenty of applicants, but they don't know who the good candidates are—which is why personal recommendations matter so much. Many places promote from within or hire based on referrals because they're scared of an unknown commodity. Your network can help get your resume noticed. "Someone you don't know will forward your resume to someone you don't know," says Republican operative Mike Shields. "Work the system. As former Congressman Bill Thomas says, 'The who beats the what.' "

Expand Your Base

Go to as many political events as possible—happy hours, fundraisers, lunches, and trainings. If they charge admission and you can't afford to go, ask if you can volunteer. Work local politicians and their aides for contacts when starting out; they're always looking for new talent. Campaign veteran Paul Lhevine notes, "I was a habitual networker. I would schedule two breakfasts in the mornings, the first at 7 a.m. followed by a second at 8 a.m. I never missed a happy hour. As a result of networking, I never wrote a cover letter and my resume was only used to give people a sense of my skill sets." And Jill Habig says, "I went to events for Howard Dean in 2003 and then started volunteering at finance events. I met the Finance Director that way and, a few months after I started volunteering, got a job."

It helps to be seen at these events, as connectors will then see you as someone in the know who can help them down the line. Networking is a two-way street; find a way to add value to the people who help you. Be memorable (in a good way). Leave people with a story or an anecdote to remember you by; I'm not great at remembering names, but I'll remember where someone is from or who they worked for last cycle.

At events, graciously and politely work the room. Have your "60-second spot" down (some call this an elevator pitch). You want to tell people you're looking without being overly aggressive. People can spot desperation, so get your game face on. Always have a good attitude, smile, and be confident. Excuse yourself from a long talker by going to the restroom, getting another drink, or saying you see someone you need to talk to (but make sure you actually know them!). Set a goal for each social event: How many people do you want to talk to? Is there someone specific you need an introduction to? Wing(wo)men are critical; bring someone with you who knows lots of people or who can come with you when you introduce yourself to a stranger.

Print up business cards with your name and contact information if you don't already have them; simple is fine. There are cheap online sites like VistaPrint or templates you can buy at Staples.com to print at home. If you have one, include a link to your LinkedIn profile or Twitter account. If you're looking for a job with labor or even Democratic campaigns in strong labor states, union printing your business cards can be well worth the additional cost.

Then pass out business cards freely; it's practically a pastime in DC. When you get a business card, discreetly write down what you talked to the person about on the back of their card. This will help you follow up the next day (and you *will* follow up the next day).

And don't get drunk at events; stick to one drink per hour. Remember, you're networking, not socializing.

Follow Up

After meeting someone new, add him or her to your contact spreadsheet and send an email with your resume attached. Briefly re-state your "60 second spot" and any help that person may have offered. If they don't reply, follow the rule of threes—after three contacts over three weeks, wait another three weeks and try again.

Veteran Democratic consultant Patrick Baskette notes, "The biggest mistake job seekers make is not working their network. I cannot count the number of times good job seekers work hard to see me once and then disappeared. Stay in touch with your network." A good trick is to send an updated resume, ask about volunteering at an upcoming event your contact is attending, or inquire about a particular organization or campaign you are researching. Ask what social events are coming up or what organizations you should join to network.

Keep contacts posted on the status of your search, if you land any interviews, and once you take a job. Fundraiser Laura Fruge makes an important point, "Keep your contacts fresh by continually reaching out to them, even if it's just to grab a cup of coffee and catch up. Use your network when you don't need anything at all."

Work Your Existing Networks

College alumni networks are a great tool for finding your next job. Use all the resources available – online databases, alumni happy hours, informational interviews – to aid you in your search. Some schools are better at this than others, but even a grad from '72 who doesn't know you will take your call or answer your email because of a shared college experience. Join relevant professional organizations (do a Google search). They usually have a young professional membership rate or will let you check out an event before joining. Contacts you meet here can be helpful in securing informational interviews and for salary research, too.

What other existing networks do you have? Are you a member of a fraternity or sorority? A local church or synagogue? A softball league or book club? Check out these organization's websites, read the bios of board members, call other friends with your affiliation, and ask around. Any kind of personal connection is a big plus and people want to help those with similar interests!

Trainings

Not only are political trainings a great way to expand your skill set, they're fantastic places to meet new people. Be sure to connect with fellow trainees as well as trainers, speakers, moderators, and event staff. There are campaign and issue trainings on both sides of the aisle, along with non-partisan trainings for demographic groups like women and LGBTQ candidates.

Here are just a few to get you started:

Non-Partisan/Bi-Partisan
- Sorensen Institute, www.sorenseninstitute.org
- America's Opportunity Fund, www.americasopportunityfund.com (candidates of color)
- Gay & Lesbian Victory Fund, www.victoryfund.org (gay and lesbian candidates)

Non-Partisan/Bi-Partisan (for women):
- Women's Campaign Fund, www.wcfonline.org
- Running Start, www.runningstartonline.org
- The White House Project, www.thewhitehouseproject.org
- National Women's Political Caucus, www.nwpc.org

Democrats/Progressives:
- Democratic GAIN, www.democraticgain.org
- Wellstone Action and Campus Camp Wellstone, www.wellstone.org
- EMILY's List and Campaign Corps, www.emilyslist.org (for women)
- Emerge America, www.emergeamerica.org (for women)
- Progressive Majority, www.progressivemajority.org
- Democracy for America, www.democracyforamerica.com
- Young Democrats of America, www.yda.org
- College Democrats of America, www.collegedemocrats.org

Republicans/Conservatives:
- The Leadership Institute, www.leadershipinstitute.org
- American Majority, www.americanmajority.org
- WISH List, www.thewishlist.org (for women)
- Susan B. Anthony List, www.sba-list.org (for women)
- Young Republicans National Federation, www.yrnf.org
- College Republican National Federation, www.crnc.org

Intern to Paid

Taking an unpaid (or, even better, a paid!) internship is a great way to expand your skills and your network. You need to be willing to work for free to prove your value. Tell an employer that you'd really like a paid position but are willing to intern to see if it's a good fit. Once you display a good attitude and a willingness to get things done, it's likely they'll try to find the money to keep you. "I started volunteering for Senator Kerry's PAC (The Citizen Soldier Fund) in 2002," says campaign veteran Carrie James. "I would go in one night a week to call Iowa and New Hampshire and then after a few months I started going two nights a week, then three nights a week and a Saturday afternoon. In January of 2003, they offered me a job." You should also consider joining your dream organization in a less than stellar role to get a foot in the door. Many organizations promote from within.

But you have to prove yourself to land the job. You can't skate by on simply being present. Capitol Hill Chief of Staff Erik Olson notes, "There are three kinds of interns: great interns who work hard and go above and beyond, who we love and then hire later; sufficient interns who punch in and out and do the work, but whose names we don't remember after six months; and horrible interns we remember forever for the wrong reasons." Which do you want to be?

Your previous internship employers should be one of the first places you look for permanent work, as well. They know you, you know them, and it takes some of the guess work out of the expectations game. Matt Singer, co-founder of Forward Montana, notes, "Volunteer and network. Network by volunteering. My first political job came out of volunteering. My second political job came out of networking."

Online Sites

Websites like Democratic GAIN, unionjobs.com, tommanatosjobs. com, and workforcongress.com all list numerous political jobs from around the country. Party committees (national and state) usually list openings on their websites and collect resumes for campaigns. There are also many listservs on various sides of the aisle or for particular jobs, like the Hill or nonprofits. Political bloggers in your state may also list (or know of) openings so read them often and follow them on Twitter.

Publications like *Roll Call, The Hill,* and *Politico* often list mid-to-senior level DC jobs and *Taegan Goddard's Political Wire* also maintains a bi-partisan, national job bank. The George Washington University Graduate School of Political Management has an exhaustive list of job websites and listservs (DC-focused but many list state jobs as well): www.gspm.org/jobs.

Searching these sites regularly is a great way to stay up on current openings and many allow you to set up daily email alerts. But everyone else out there is also applying to these jobs, so don't count on job sites alone; Tom Manatos' list, for instance, has over 21,000 subscribers. Do some additional homework and find the original posting (particularly if the listing doesn't list the representative or campaign; just Google the job description to see if it pops up elsewhere) so you can apply directly.

Beware the big, paid sites. Since many political jobs are never posted in the first place, they likely won't post on sites like Monster.com. You may be able to find some local nonprofit, labor or association jobs via these sites or those connected to your local newspaper but don't spend too much time wading through the myriad of jobs that will come back in your search. A good way to weed out unwanted postings is a keyword search with "political," "advocacy," or other relevant terms.

Find a Mentor

Finally, you want someone on your side, who can give you unfiltered, trusted advice. In short, you want a mentor.

But you can't waltz up to someone with similar interests and a career path you crave and ask, "Will you be my mentor?" It's more informal than that. Ideally, you want someone like you but a few steps ahead on the career ladder. If someone takes a particular liking to you and really wants to help, take them up on any offer. Keep your guard up a little for ulterior motives, but usually a potential mentor just sees someone they can help.

Having a network of mentors is really the best way to go, so you're not relying on one person's advice. This will happen over time as you become close to former co-workers and supervisors. Remember that it's a two-way street (help them when you can) and you need to nurture these relationships when you're not job hunting as well. Mentors and skills are the keys to longevity in politics.

Christy Agner says that she not only had strong mentors along the way but "I'm always looking for good people to bring up behind me, smart up and comers." This is particularly true for women; find a mentor and be a mentor. Once you're more established in your career, extend the hand back!

You need support from friends, too. "Everyone needs a sounding board – someone a rung or two higher up on the ladder that you can talk to and ask the dumb questions," says campaign vet Hayley Zachary. EMILY's List Executive Director Amy Dacey notes, "I also have my kitchen cabinet, my team of peers who have my back; we can share experiences as our careers move along together." And former campaign staffer Michelle Study notes, "The friendships that I have made in my political career still serve me today! These are lifelong friendships that create a network that will support you well into your future careers."

The Political Ladder:
- ✓ Make a list of contacts and track them in a spreadsheet
- ✓ Get business cards printed
- ✓ Go to as many political events as possible
- ✓ Use trainings as networking opportunities
- ✓ Find a mentor and be a mentor

GETTING NOTICED: COVER LETTERS, WRITING SAMPLES, AND REFERENCES

Now it's time to make the case that you're the best person for the job. The traditional ways to do this are through cover letters, writing samples, and references. I'll help you put together these important pieces of the job application puzzle, and also tell you how to campaign for the job.

Cover Letters

Once you're in the door, you may never have to formally apply for a job again; people will steal you away. A good friend of mine with a prominent political job hasn't written a cover letter since 2006.

Until then, however, you need a way to tell your story. Your cover letter should paint a picture of your experience and discuss why you're interested in a particular job. It should not just reiterate your resume, which is easier said than done.

Most importantly, for most jobs, your cover letter is your writing sample. It needs to be perfect. "Writing and communicating are the most important skills. Most people think they're good at writing, but on average are not," says Mag Gottlieb of The George Washington University's Graduate School of Political Management. "Take a continuing education or community college class to demonstrate that you know how to write."

Do Your Homework

While you should have a generic cover letter on hand, it's critical to tailor every cover letter to a particular job and company. Generic cover letters don't cut it in my book, and I usually don't bother to look at the resume attached.

Every cover letter should take you at least an hour to research and write. Go on the company's website and read up. Maybe you're already familiar with their work, but it's important to know about new initiatives, press releases, news articles, and any major staff changes. Then incorporate your research into your cover letter to demonstrate you know your stuff and want the job.

Read job descriptions carefully! When people write them, they think long and hard about the type of person they're looking for and the skill set they need. These job descriptions are your clue sheets; think about how your past experiences and skills fit in with what they're looking for in an employee. Make a side-by-side list of the skills desired in the job description and your qualifications with examples. If there's no job description for this particular job, tailor your cover letter to their anticipated needs; do some online research and try to find descriptions for similar jobs.

If you're emailing your resume and cover letter via a "jobs@" email address, try to find another way to submit materials as well, such as the head of the department or a human resources staffer. Those generic email addresses are an abyss into which your application disappears. Ask friends, use LinkedIn, and go to the organization's website to find an appropriate name to which you can address your cover letter.

Easy as One, Two, Three

First off, your cover letter should never be more than one page. Dig deep and recall those fourth grade lessons on writing a formal business letter. Your cover letter should include your name and contact information on top, then the name and contact information of the person to whom you are addressing, followed by the date and a greeting. Look at the examples here for formatting and content ideas.

Sample Cover Letters

Jill Jones

222 Miller Rd • Washington, DC 12345 • (202) 555-9876 • jilljones@gmail.com

September 24, 2010

Julia Norman, President

Family Partnerships USA

9876 Connecticut Avenue NW, Suite 123

Washington, DC 20009

Dear Ms. Norman:

With more than ten years of experience in the U.S House of Representatives in various positions, including Legislative Director and health, education and labor advisor, I am an ideal candidate for the position of Outreach Manager.

In my capacity as Legislative Director for Congressman Joe Donaldson, I managed a staff of five legislative aides and was responsible for implementing and overseeing the Congressman's legislative and appropriations priorities. I have drafted more than ten pieces of legislation, including five that have been enacted into law. During my ten years of Congressional service, I developed exceptional written and oral communications skills and a strong ability to multitask and accomplish directives in a high-pressure environment. I am also particularly skilled at developing long-term legislative initiatives as well as more timely ideas or "quick hits" in response to salient issues or media interest. I am adept at not only developing new ideas, but at carefully analyzing the politics of an issue to determine how and when to move forward with a proposal.

In addition to my management duties, I served as the Congressman's primary policy and political advisor on all aspects of health, education, and labor policy, including both appropriations and authorizing committee work. As the lead staffer responsible for monitoring health care reform efforts in both the House and Senate, I advocated for the Congressman's priorities as the legislation moved through the process with leadership and committee staff and met with constituents to convey the Congressman's views on this critical issue. I also facilitated public forums for the Congressman to interact with constituents relating to health care reform, including round-tables, stakeholder meetings, conference calls and telephone town halls.

My management experience, creativity, and proven record of accomplishment with Congressman Donaldson would be a great asset to Family Partnerships USA. I look forward to the opportunity to explain in greater detail how I can make a significant contribution to your team and can be reached at jilljones@gmail.com. Thank you for your consideration.

Sincerely,

Jill Jones

November 30, 2008

Henry Kurt

Senator-Elect Joe Donaldson

Sent via email to hkurt@donaldson.com

Dear Mr. Kurt:

I am interested in the Scheduling position in the Washington, D.C. Office for United States Senator-Elect Joe Donaldson. This position is a unique opportunity for me to use my experience in congressional and executive level scheduling to help the Senator serve the people of my home state. Senator Donaldson will need a Scheduler with Washington, D.C. experience and a strong work ethic to get him and his staff started in the United States Senate. As a native of Townsville, Ontario, it would be an honor for me to fill that role and help him accomplish great things for Ontario.

Based on my experience as a Scheduler for a new Member of Congress, a former Cabinet Member, and presidential candidates, I know that you are looking for a Scheduler who can handle the challenge of being attentive to official and political requests while constantly remaining sensitive to the Senator's personal time with his family. As Scheduler for Former Secretary John Doe and Congresswoman June Goldman of Toronto, I strengthened my ability to balance the opportunities important to them, both personally and professionally, in order to make the most effective use of their time. As a staffer on two presidential campaigns, I had to be flexible yet focused, as my skills for managing logistics were put to the test in a fast paced, multi-tasked environment. The organizational and communication skills that I learned in these different environments are crucial to maintaining a seamless scheduling system for Senator Donaldson.

I am confident of the skills and experience I have to offer as a Scheduler in the Washington, D.C. office of Senator-Elect Donaldson. Please let me know if there is anything else I can provide to you and I look forward to talking with you in the near future.

Sincerely,

Jamie Ryan
Enclosure: Resume

Blueprint Executive Search

Attention: Ana Morales, Search Principal

Via email: ana@blueprintstaffing.com

May 18, 2010

Dear Ms. Morales,

I am writing to express my interest in becoming the Executive Director/CEO of the Ontario Improvement Fund. I learned of the opening from several community contacts and have discussed the organization extensively with peers as well as with Board Chairman Bill Weiss.

My experience and skill set match your need for a visionary leader who can build on the Ontario Improvement Fund's many successes. As Executive Director at the Canadian Environmental League, I gained valuable expertise in staff management, program evaluation, strategic planning, budgeting, and Board relations. This challenging experience, after having managed other national programs, further developed my leadership style; I believe in a collaborative atmosphere and a results-driven culture. It also evolved my philosophy on philanthropic giving: donors want to know how their contribution is making an impact and often desire to be part of the change they seek. Central to both my leadership style and giving philosophy is the importance of establishing strategic goals – organizations cannot achieve success unless that success is clearly defined and each aspect of your work strives to meet your goals.

My background in social entrepreneurship management and political expertise will provide the Ontario Improvement Fund with a unique approach. Politics is inherently results-driven – there are winners and losers, defined timelines and tight budgets. I know how to achieve much with little, and how to pass those skills on to staff, members, and partner organizations. Over my varied career, I have worked directly with students, lawyers, donors, international activists, politicians, constituents, and the press. I know I can use these past experiences to grow the Ontario Improvement Fund's network of members. I also possess excellent oral and written communications skills, including extensive media and training experience.

I am excited by the possibility of joining the Ontario Improvement Fund team. Please find my resume attached. I look forward to discussing the Executive Director/CEO position with you further in person.

Sincerely,

Jamie Ryan

The bulk of your letter can be summed up in three main paragraphs and a closing:

- Introduction: Who are you, how did you hear about this job, and a one-sentence qualifications summary about why your skills match this job.
- Your experience: Here's where you go into detail about your past work experience. Rather than re-stating your resume, group things by skill set (managing staff and volunteers, fund-raising, working on a team) or tell a story that exemplifies who you are as an employee. Was there a difficult assignment you worked hard on and surpassed expectations? A challenging event you had to organize? Tell your story in terms future employers will understand and appreciate.
- Skills + Job = Me: Look carefully at those job descriptions and think about how to map your past skills and experience to their needs. You may want to pull out three or four bullets from the job description and address them specifically. This part of your cover letter should emphasize why *you* are right for *this* particular job.
- Closing: This should be a pleasant, generic sentence to thank the employer and state your availability for an in-person interview.

Remember, your cover letter should be perfect. Use 11 or 12 point font and an easy to read font style that matches your resume. Simple, direct writing is best – it's not a vocab quiz. Be professional – use correct grammar and spelling and don't rely only on spell check. Some people will skim your letter (yes, skim, not read) to get a better sense of you as a potential employee, but really, they're just making sure you can put a coherent sentence together.

Finally, if you're emailing your application, your email to the employer is your cover letter and you should structure it as such.

References

Choose your references carefully; they can be a huge asset to your job search and your ongoing networking efforts. Start off by making a list of everyone who could be a reference. This should include your direct supervisor for each job, their supervisor, college professors (if you're a recent grad), and a few co-workers.

Sample References

References for Jamie Ryan

David Goldman
Director, Canada for Obama
(321) 555-9132 cell
dgoldman@obama.can

Jarrell Humphreys
Director, Canadians United
Former Field Director, Ontario for Obama
(654) 555-7586 cell
jhumphreys@bmail.com

Kate Solomon
Political Director, Environment Ontario
(987) 555-2771 cell
ksolomon@bmail.com

Ideally, each reference was your supervisor in some capacity. Your day-to-day supervisor (for instance, the field director if you were an organizer or the legislative director if you were an intern or junior staffer on the Hill) knows more about your work and can speak more directly to who you are as an employee than the campaign manager or Chief of Staff. This is a huge help to future employers. If you don't list your supervisor, you need to have a good reason and an explanation. Employers know not everyone gets along famously, particularly in tense campaign situations. Never bad mouth anyone, but be prepared to answer questions about past bosses.

Only list the candidate, elected official, executive director, or other big name if you worked with them directly on a daily basis. The exception to this rule is the personal relationship. Chances are someone you worked with knows someone at the organization or campaign to which you are applying. In that case, your contact and their relationship may come in handy and you can list them as well.

Narrow your list of references depending on the job. When in doubt, list your last three direct supervisors. You should also select references who can speak to your most relevant skill sets for this job. Remember, you only need to submit references when asked and this step usually happens when you're a finalist for a job.

Most importantly, call your references and make sure they're OK with being listed. Ask a few questions to make sure they'll say good things about your work. A good question is, "Do you have the time to give me a positive reference?" It's a nice little wink to get someone off the hook if they are uncomfortable giving you a reference or are too busy to call someone back. Get their most up-to-date contact information and inquire how they prefer to be reached (work phone, cell phone, or email).

You should prep each reference if you think a future employer will be calling. Email your references the job description, your cover letter, and your most updated resume for the job. Suggest things for them to stress and provide talking points for any missteps. What are your weaknesses for the job and how can a former boss address that weakness? What skills do you want to shine through? Reference checks aren't perfunctory – they can reinforce feelings (positively or negatively), or help change someone's mind.

Writing Samples

You really only need to submit a writing sample when asked, and it should never be more than three pages (except if you're told otherwise). Unless you're applying for policy-wonk jobs, college papers are not appropriate, and even then, cut it down.

Try to submit a writing sample that is relevant to the job. For a press or communications job, submit press releases – or write one as an example. You can draft advocacy emails, fundraising solicitations, constituent letters, white papers, and more to demonstrate your writing capabilities and creativity.

Again, your writing sample needs to be perfect – no spelling or grammatical errors. Have a friend (or five) read it over to make sure spell check didn't miss something.

Campaign for It!

If this is your dream job, consider having a reference or two proactively call an employer on your behalf, particularly if they have a connection to the organization or campaign. Tom Manatos notes, "Employers want recommendations from someone they trust. Try to have multiple validators get you the interview and the job offer." Don't overuse this privilege though – you only want to call in a favor with references when it's a job you'll definitely take if offered. Hailey Snow, who has worked for several large advocacy groups, had a well-connected boss call around when she was up for two jobs. "He is a big deal with senior staff at both organizations and he pushed really hard for me, making multiple calls on my behalf," she says.

You can also have friends and former co-workers help you. If they work at the organization or know someone there, ask them to pass on your resume and cover letter with a recommendation.

Submitting Materials

Unless otherwise instructed, put your name in the file name (such as FirstName LastName Resume) and your cover letter in the same format. When in doubt, submit as a .pdf. Follow every instruction when applying for a job online; they're looking for petty reasons to disqualify people and something as simple as not using their pre-ferred subject line may kick your application to the curb.

The Political Ladder:
- ✓ Create a perfect, triple spell-checked generic cover letter
- ✓ Make a list of potential references with current contact information
- ✓ Compile possible writing samples or create your own

LANDING THE JOB: INTERVIEWS AND SALARY NEGOTIATIONS

Interviews are the key to getting the job. They are (usually) your first face-to-face encounter and the most meaningful way to prove yourself. You need to come with your A-game; be prepared and professional.

There are two general types of interviews – informational and for a particular job. No matter which one you're preparing for, there are some basic factors to take into account and ways to prepare.

Finally, when you get the offer, you need to negotiate salary. This is many people's least favorite part of the process but key to your long-term success.

Informational Interviews

You've read about how important networking is to your job search. Informational interviews are an integral part of expanding your network and building deeper relationships with contacts and potential employers. They are also low-pressure, and a great way to feel out a company or organization and for them to feel you out, too. "They may not have an immediate job for you," notes communications expert Jessica Smith. "But meeting a contact in person gives you a leg up over a candidate who is just a name on a resume, allows people to invest in you (and they might be more inclined to think of you when they hear about an opening) and it may lead to other networking opportunities or leads." It's a great way to get insider information about a company and what they may ask you in a formal interview setting.

Set up interviews with any contacts your network has put you in touch with, or do some online research to figure out who has your dream job. Most people want to help job seekers and even the busiest person has 15 minutes. Your best bet may be a former employee who is willing to dish. Start off by emailing your contact a version of your "60-second spot" along with your resume to request a meeting. Be specific about why you'd like to talk—if you're looking for career advice, trying to decide between two different paths, or even if you don't have a career focus but you heard that he or she is really smart and successful, say it. Be flexible with your timing and be sure to offer to meet the person at his or her office or location of choice.

Follow the rule of threes: send an initial email. If your contact doesn't follow up within a week, pick up the phone. Mention that you sent an email last week and would like half an hour or even just 15 minutes to pick his or her brain about job opportunities. If that doesn't do the trick, wait another week and call or email again. After three forms of contact over three weeks, wait another three weeks and try again. It's not personal, people are just busy.

You can also have a mutual friend introduce you over email (you can use LinkedIn to help you find contacts). Send your friend an updated resume and an email script they can cut and paste or adapt slightly to introduce you to your informational interview target. That extra personal contact will likely guarantee a reply.

Once you get the meeting, treat the informational interview like a regular interview and pull out all the stops. Start by dressing the part; if you're meeting at a coffee shop, a suit isn't necessary but business casual is appropriate. If your meeting is at an office that maintains professional business attire, for example a law firm, wear a suit. Be early, not on time. Always be polite and professional even when you know the person you're meeting.

Take advantage of the time you have. Start with your "60-second spot"—what you want and how they can help. You're not there to explicitly ask for a job, just their advice. Knowing how someone wants to help is almost as important as the help they provide. Ask specific, directed questions to guide the conversation. Will they proactively connect you to people in interesting jobs or organizations? Pass on jobs they hear about? Should you to email them every few weeks or call them once a month? Or do they want to contact you?

After the informational interview, email a thank you note along with the most updated version of your resume. Also send a handwritten thank you note summarizing what you discussed. "I'm always amazed at how few people write a note after an informational interview," notes lobbyist Julie Philp. "I recommend that you write thank yous right after the meeting and hand deliver the note, particularly if you meet with someone who works on the Hill or the government, since security screenings slow down mail delivery." If your interviewer connects you to other contacts, reply or follow-up right away; you don't want to burn a bridge or come off as a flake. Remember to track everyone in your contacts spreadsheet. Also let your connector know that you met their contact and appreciate the introduction.

If you're lucky enough to get a formal job interview as a result of an informational meeting, seek your contact's advice about the company or person with who you are interviewing. And once you secure a position, notify your contacts via email, and for anyone who went above and beyond, send another handwritten thank you note.

Phone Interviews

Phone interviews are very tough for both the interviewer and interviewee. It is, however, a great way to even the playing field for applicants from all over the country, so be prepared for your first round interview to be conducted over the phone.

First, set up an appointment to talk so you're not blind-sided by the phone call—find out if you are supposed to call them or if they will be calling you. If the latter, make sure your phone is on the "ring" setting and that you're ready for the call ahead of time. Make sure to find a quiet place to talk—do not conduct an interview for another job at your current place of work.

As with in-person interviews, it's fine to have notes, print outs, and prepared questions and answers in front of you to refer to throughout. You should take notes about what you're asked. You may also want to find an interview spot with access to the Internet so you can answer any questions that arise; have your computer handy but minimize your browser and close your email to avoid distraction.

For video interviews, you'll also need a quiet, professional-looking space. Test the sound and picture quality beforehand. Dress the part – remember, they can see you.

In-Person Interviews

Preparing for Your Interview

First, relax! You got the interview – clearly, the company or organization sees something in you they like. Be confident in your abilities and know that the interview process is a way for the employer to figure out the right person for the job.

Second, always remember it's not about you; it's about them. This is particularly hard to do when you're unemployed or have been searching for a long time. You want it to be about how badly you want this job, how badly you *need* this job. Frankly, my dear, they don't give a damn. Interviews are about learning how you will make their lives easier if they hire you for the job.

There are a few questions your potential employer is looking to answer: do you fit with this company, organization, or campaign? In what role? And would you do a good job? You need to prepare adequately to answer these questions and more. Ultimately there are likely several people who are qualified for the job, but the employer is looking for the best fit. In politics, staffs can be small, so office culture matters. And hiring for political jobs is, well, political. It may not even come down to who is best for the job, but rather, who had the best contacts.

The first key to a successful job interview is research, research, research. Who is the candidate's opponent? What was the Democratic or Republican performance in the district for the last race? For organizations, who are the other players in the field, (for example, if you were interviewing with Toyota, you'd also want to research Honda) and do they work as a coalition or are they considered competition? You need to know this organization, candidate, association or think tank better than they know themselves. Read their website top to bottom and take appropriate notes. Set up an RSS feed to get recent news. Follow relevant staff, competitors, and media outlets covering the industry on Twitter. Ask for the names of the person or people you'll be interviewing with as well as titles/roles so you can do some research; Google and LinkedIn are helpful here. On the day of your interview, check all relevant news and social media outlets and review the organization's website for any breaking news.

Next, plan it out. Map the location of your interview and see how long it will take to get there. If you're unfamiliar with the area, do a test run. Drive to the location a few days ahead of time at the same time of day you'll be driving there for the interview. You can never be too early on the big day. Find a nearby coffee shop or other location where you can hang out before your scheduled interview time. Know where you're going to park and how much it costs.

Finally, prep for your interview. You can guess what they're going to ask, so prepare answers to those easy to foresee questions by writing them out—questions and answers. Think of them as your interview talking points. Also have talking points for each job you've held, including what you learned and how that experience is applicable to the job you are applying for now (this is often called the resume walk-through).

Just like a political candidate, use your own version of a "60-second spot"—a brief overview of your experience and skills and why you're right for the job (some people call this the elevator pitch). Write it down and practice it out loud in front of friends. If you're shy, practice until you're comfortable talking about yourself and projecting confidence.

Ultimately though, what every interview question is really getting at is: why are you the best person for the job? All of your answers should directly or indirectly answer that question.

You should also prep for likely questions related to the specific job. Look at the job description and outline how your experience matches each qualification. Maybe you don't fit each need; know where your weaknesses lie and how you'll overcome or compensate for them in this position. Think back to how you prepared to write your cover letter—review your side-by-side list of skills desired in the job description and your qualifications with examples.

For helpful interview tips, I highly recommend Gayle Laakmann McDowell's "Behavioral Preparation Grid," downloadable from www.thegoogleresume.com as well as Job Interviews for Dummies by Joyce Lain Kennedy.

Sample Interview Questions

These are typical questions asked in an interview. Remember, prepare your answers ahead of time!

- Why are you interested in this job?

- Why would you be good at this job?

- What past experience would you draw on to excel in this job?

- What are your strengths and weaknesses? ("I just work so hard, I don't know when to stop!" is not a weakness. You need real problems and answers, with talking points on how you've made progress to improve on weaknesses.)

- How do you work within a team?

- What are you like as a leader?

- What is your management style?

- What do you like in a manager?

- Where do you see yourself in five years?

- What's your dream job?

- Why are you leaving your current position?

- How would friends or colleagues describe you?

- Tell me about a challenging time or circumstance.

- Describe how you've dealt with a challenging co-worker or boss.

- What accomplishment are you most proud of?

- What activities do you enjoy in your spare time?

For Students:

- What would you do differently if you could go to college all over again?

For Career Switchers:

- Why this industry/field/campaign/organization? Why now?

It's also important to prepare questions to ask your interviewer. Obvious questions will likely be answered during the interview process, so prepare open-ended questions to get beyond the basics.

Here are some examples:
- What makes a person successful in this job?
- Can you describe a typical day or week in this position?
- What should I do from day one to be successful in this position?
- What's your favorite thing about working here?
- What staff training is available to help me expand my skill set?

What Not to Wear

Your appearance matters—particularly if you're in a public role or representing a public figure—so you may need to invest in one or two interview outfits. For guys, this generally means a suit and tie with a dress shirt and nice shoes. For less formal situations, like a campaign interview, khakis, dress shirt, sport coat, and tie are usually appropriate. And no loud or inappropriate ties. For women, dress pants or a skirt with a classic sweater set or blouse is usually fine for more informal interviews, but a suit is best otherwise. Don't overdo it on makeup, perfume, jewelry, cleavage, short skirts, or overly high heels. For both men and women, jeans, flip-flops, and tank tops are also no-nos on an interview or at a networking event.

Everything should be clean, neat, and wrinkle free. Iron your clothes and polish your shoes the night before; do a dry cleaning run, if need be—it's worth the same day cost. Take out unusual piercings and don't flaunt tattoos. Over-dressed and conservative are always better than inappropriate and underdressed. Like it or not, a job interview is not the time to express your fashionista personality or unique sense of style. This dress code should be applied to political events and your first few days of work as well, until you get a feel for your new office's norms.

You also need a professional handbag, messenger bag, or briefcase as well as a new folder or portfolio to hold any notes and copies of your resume.

The Big Day

It sounds obvious, but try to get a good night's sleep the night before. Arrive at the office at least 15 minutes ahead of your interview time. Allow five minutes to get through security and make your way to the reception area. Since you did a test run, you should know exactly how long it takes to get there; be sure to build in extra time for unforeseen emergencies.

Bring several copies of your resume to give to your inteviewer(s) as well as a copy of your cover letter and the job description for your reference. Also print out your questions or write them legibly on your notepad, which you should use to take notes on during the interview. It's fine to refer to notes and take notes throughout. Finally, bring breath mints and pop a few before you arrive on-site.

During your pre-interview time, review your talking points, questions, and anything you've printed out about the organization (such as bios, mission statement, or press releases). It's helpful to review materials just before you head in so everything is fresh in your mind.

Smile. Be polite and friendly. Use a firm handshake. Be aware of nervous habits: sit up straight, make eye contact, and don't pick at your nails or fuss with your hair. Watch the "Um's" (this is also a nervous habit—practice and prepare, and you'll feel more confident in your answers).

It's tough to do when you're nervous, but be sure to listen! What your interviewer says is every bit as important as what you say. Listen for red flags like high turnover, new and inexperienced managers, family members on staff (particularly for campaigns), and fundraising or budgetary concerns. Your interviewer may also drop hints about what the organization is looking for, why the last person left this position, or your perceived weaknesses for the job (which you can then address).

The interview will likely start off with your "60-second spot," the resume walk-through, and typical questions. You should be well prepared for these parts so relax and answer each question thoroughly and thoughtfully. Play to your strengths and answer any concerns they may have about prior experience. Mike Shields, a former campaign manager and Chief of Staff on the Hill, says "Take advantage of open-ended, softball questions. Be aggressive with what they need to know about you." Most importantly, remember that there are rarely correct answers in the interview process; employers are trying to get a sense of you, your experience, and how you would react to likely circumstances. Keep in mind that your interviewer may test how you react to stressful circumstances by purposefully throwing you hardball questions.

Once the basics are covered, be prepared for things to get more complicated. For instance, job interviewers can't outright ask you about your political beliefs, but they may ask cover questions about your favorite politician or which websites or periodicals you read to get a sense of your partisan affiliation. Note that it is illegal for employers to ask your age, gender, race, national origin, religion, marital/family status, or whether you have any disabilities.

You may also get questions about specific job circumstances. If you left a job under less than stellar conditions, prepare your answers. A classic example is if you worked for a notoriously difficult boss. There's no need to badmouth anyone; it's a small world and comments will come back to bite you. The best answer here is something like, "It was a challenging work environment and I learned a lot. I think I'm ready to handle any situation."

Never bring up money first (more on this to follow). Disclose things like planned vacations or a potential conflict of interest after a second interview.

Close by asking about the company's hiring process and timeline. Ask if there are additional materials you can provide to help the decision-making process. Be sure to get a business card from everyone you interviewed with so you know how to spell names for your thank you notes.

After the interview, like many people you'll likely focus on everything you messed up. That's normal; try not to worry about it. You should, however, self-evaluate your interview. Look back on your notes and reflect on questions you were asked so you can plan and practice your answers for next time.

Follow-Up

Send a thank you email right away and then send a handwritten note. The notes should recap your enthusiasm and qualifications for the job. Be sure to send any additional information asked for, such as references or a writing sample, in a timely manner.

Sample Thank You Notes

After a first interview, to an acquaintance

Dear Rhonda,

Thank you for taking the time to meet with me on May 5th regarding the open position at XYZ. I am grateful for your willingness to discuss all aspects of the job as well as my ability to fit into the XYZ's DC office. I look forward to working with you and Stefan in the future!

Sincerely,

Jill Jones

After a first interview, to a new contact

Dear Stefan,

Thank you very much for considering me for a position with the XYZ. I enjoyed talking to you and Rhonda Goldman on May 5th. Your comments gave me a good understanding of the expectations for the legislative position I am seeking. I am confident that my background and experience working on the Hill and my ability to excel in a team-oriented environment could be useful to the XYZ.

Sincerely,

Jill Jones

After a second interview

Mr. Schwartz,

I wanted to send you a quick note to thank you for meeting with me on May 16th. I found our conversation to be very refreshing, and I appreciate your openness and honesty.

I am very excited about the chance to work with such a great team. This position at XYZ is exactly what I have been looking for, and I sincerely hope I am the person you are looking for as well. If you have any questions or concerns, please feel free to contact me at 202-456-1234. Thank you once again, and I look forward to talking further.

With great interest,

Jill Jones

Getting the Offer and Salary Negotiations

Everyone negotiates salary so don't be embarrassed. It's always the most awkward part of an interview. Many employers won't even bring up salary until a second interview, when they know you're a finalist. Asking for your own salary is somehow harder than asking other people for a donation or to volunteer. But what's the worst that can happen? Someone says no? Whatever. Find a compromise and move on. However, it is important to calculate what your salary and benefits requirements are before you interview, so you know what you can and cannot accept. For help, use the Salary Math worksheet.

Salary Math

Calculating your baseline salary is an important step in determining your next job. First, make a list of all of your monthly expenses (as well as annual expenses that you may pay all at once, like car insurance). Next, compile all of your credit card and related statements or bills from the past three months so you can average out your food and entertainment expenses. Then create a graph with your basics.

Here's an example. Let's call this person Jill:

ITEM	MONTHLY	ANNUAL
Rent	$1,200	$14,400
Car payment	$300	$3,600
Car insurance	$50	$600
Gas	$60	$720
Cell phone	$75	$900
Student loan	$250	$3,000
Food	$400	$4,800
Entertainment	$300	$3,600
TOTAL	$2,635	$31,620

These are Jill's basic monthly expenses. Note that Jill does not have credit card debt; if you do, be sure to add in those payments as well. She can be somewhat flexible on things like food and entertainment, but this is her monthly average. Also note that this graph does not take major purchases like clothing and furniture into account. Jill is also only applying to jobs with fully covered health care; you may need to add in some uncovered expenses.

Now we account for Jill's taxes. We add roughly 25% of her basic expenses (this will vary from state to state), or $7,905 to $31,620. Voila! **Jill needs to make a minimum of $39,525.**

But Jill currently lives in Washington DC and is thinking of relocating to Columbus, Ohio, for a year to work on a campaign. According to the Motley Fool's cost of living wizard (motleyfool.salary.com), Jill can afford to take an $11,739 pay cut if she moves to Columbus, leaving her at $27,786. Jill may also secure free or discounted supporter housing, reducing her monthly rent. But she will likely spend more on gas and food, as she will work long hours.

And Jill is not planning to save any money for emergencies, periods of unemployment, and retirement – a big no-no. You should try to pad your minimum so you can set aside a few hundred dollars each month.

So, Jill should ask for $46,000-$49,000 and take nothing lower than mid-40's in DC, and in Ohio, ask for $34,000-$36,000 and take nothing below the low-30's.

You should never bring up money first; let the employer raise the question. Salary ranges may be listed on the job description or you may be able to do some online research to get a range, particularly for government and campaign jobs where expenses are public. You can hedge and say your needs depend on the entire package (health care, cell phone reimbursement, vacation days, flex time, etc.). Discussing your salary history is a nice way to dodge the discussion and justify what you're asking for. Be sure to let the employer know if you're changing locations (and need money for a higher cost of living) or if you were given additional responsibility in a prior job.

If pressed for a number, you need to give a number. Say it, and then shut up. Wait for their reply. Expect a counter offer and know whether you can accept it. You usually only get one counter offer and it's take it or leave it. Never give a salary below what you would accept. Realize that the highest number you say is the max they will ever go to, so start off higher than you would expect to get. Don't invent a competing opportunity or job offer with a higher salary to strengthen your negotiating position; again, politics is a small world and this can backfire.

If the company can't match your ideal salary, can you get a title bump? Titles are free! Large organizations and corporate jobs often can't negotiate on titles but smaller organizations and campaigns likely can. Those same organizations and campaigns have smaller budgets and less wiggle room to negotiate salaries though, so know when a final answer is a final answer.

Your salary may also depend on your location; money goes further in small towns and cities vs. expensive cities like New York, DC, and San Francisco. There are several cost of living calculators online that you can use to determine what you need if changing locations.

Again, think about your needs vs. wants. Your decision may not come down to salary. You shouldn't take a high-paying job just because it pays well – you won't be happy in the long run. Jay Vincent, senior vice president at Saint Consulting, said, "I took a 40% pay cut to work in politics. Looking back it was well worth it because I began working with incredibly smart and driven people who helped make me a better citizen-activist." One consultant notes, "See the value in a position beyond the title and salary. People who continued at a place with more opportunity for growth have been more successful than those who took a slightly higher salary and a less interesting job." Does the organization frequently promote from within? You may be able to move up the ladder quickly once you land and prove yourself.

Women, myself included, are simply not as good at salary negotiations as men. Now, I'm not one to make generalizations like this, but it's been universally true in my observations on both sides of the negotiating table and in discussions with friends and co-workers. Campaign veteran Jackie Bray says, "I have been the lowest paid staffer out of my peers with the same role in every job I've ever had. Even as a strong woman, I just don't negotiate for myself. I train field staff on how to make a hard ask and then I fail to ask for what I deserve. We have to get over the fear of asking and be willing to negotiate for what we deserve." Politico Simone L. Ward notes, "Nice girls don't get the corner office. Don't be afraid to ask for what you want. If you don't advocate for yourself, no one else will." Find another woman a few rungs higher than you on the ladder and ask the tough questions. Mika Brzezinski, co-host of MSNBC's "Morning Joe," wrote a terrific book called <u>Knowing Your Value</u>; I highly recommend it for some inspirational girl power and advice from some of the most influential women in politics and business.

It may take days or even weeks for a prospective employer to get back to you about next steps. If the employer said they would get back to you by the end of the week, it's fine to contact them the following Monday if you still haven't heard from them. If you don't hear right away it doesn't mean you won't get the offer. People are busy and, much to your frustration, this hiring process may not be their top priority.

Once you get the offer, it's OK to take at least a day to think about it (or a little longer for non-campaign jobs). And don't make a final decision about a job until you get the formal offer. Break down money/benefits, career path/development, and happiness/personal passion. Always get the offer in writing, even if it's just an email, and also accept in writing.

If you don't take a job offer, decline politely but firmly. Renege on an offer only if you have to – these things do happen but recognize you're burning a *big* bridge.

The Political Ladder:

✓ Write and practice your "60-second spot"

✓ Buy thank you notes

✓ Set up RSS feeds and follow Twitter accounts for companies, organizations, and candidates you're interested in

✓ Write down answers to likely interview questions

✓ Invest in business attire clothing for interviews if needed or hit the dry cleaner

✓ Do your salary math

HOW TO NOT GET FIRED:
THE DAY-TO-DAY

Do your job. Sounds easy, right? But there are good ways and bad ways to do your job. When it comes to starting a new job and proving yourself, I've said it before and I'll say it again – you can't just do the minimum and expect to get ahead. Going above and beyond at the beginning is what will make you stand out. But it's also important to "stay in your lane." As in do *your* job, not mine. People can be territorial about what they consider to be their areas of responsibility. So know your place, and help co-workers out when you can. Counterintuitive, no? But it's rule number one. You need to walk a fine line. As The Rock famously said, "Know your role."

Also remember, as a friend of mine so eloquently put it, "No one knows anything about anything." So don't be intimidated. Just get to it.

Getting A Promotion

Being really good at your job can be a detriment to your advancement on campaigns and even in other circumstances; managers don't want to lose a good person in that role. You need to be aggressive in securing a promotion and watch out for your own interests.

A former boss gave me excellent advice at the end of a campaign cycle; she said, "Don't be a scheduler forever." I was a political assistant to a powerful member of Congress and much of my job consisted of coordinating the congresswoman's schedule and travel. I was good at it – well organized, adaptable, and familiar with her needs—and comfortable with my day-to-day responsibilities. Once you prove your worth in a job, it's all too easy to stay there. This is particularly true for women; they can easily get pigeonholed as assistants and schedulers for campaigns and on the Hill. Having a boss warn me against a lateral career move was critical advice at a critical time. Former campaigner Glen Roth, put it this way, "Being an assistant to a seasoned political pro is a valuable way to gain access and insight into how the process actually works. But the timing of leaving this apprenticeship is a tricky calculus — leave too early and you may not learn all you can, stay too long and your professional identity can become too tied to your boss."

Managers will often accommodate a pay raise to keep a good employee. But you need to prove yourself, just as you would in an interview. Never assume you'll get a raise at your annual review. If you do ask for a pay increase, make sure you're aware of company financials and have a reasonable ask; requesting a $10,000 raise when people are being laid off is probably not a good idea. Flexible hours, a new title (titles are free!), or additional vacation time are also good things to negotiate in lieu of or in addition to a pay raise.

Track your added value throughout the year so you don't have to scramble when it comes time for your review. If you're not required to write weekly or monthly reports, create your own. Include major accomplishments and quantify information as much as possible. Be sure to note if you saved the organization money or time, took on additional responsibilities, met a benchmark early, or exceeded expectations.

How to Not Get Fired

A few classic monikers are applicable to nearly all political jobs: expect the unexpected. Always go above and beyond. Be a team player.

The most important thing is to project a can-do, get things done attitude. You want to be seen as the "go-to" person – reliable, hard-working, and efficient. Learn what other people do in the office so you can lend a hand as needed or pinch-hit in an emergency (everything from database basics to knowing where copier paper is stored). At the same time, however, know what your "real" job is and don't get sidetracked. No matter how many extra projects you take on and how many co-workers you help, you'll still be judged on your job. While tracking your own successes, build goodwill and give credit (and thanks) to co-workers when credit is due.

Beware martyr syndrome! Being productive does not mean being the first one in, last one out every day. Especially on campaigns, this just leads to exhaustion. Take breaks during the day to avoid burnout and stay productive. Gchat, Facebook, and other websites and tools can be a major distraction; tell non-work friends that you can't chat or reply during the day or block or turn off those features while at work.

If you're not sure how to effectively complete a project, ask! Better that your boss spends a little more time explaining things upfront than you spend hours doing something wrong. Rebecca Epstein of The Management Center notes, "Get clear on your roles and goals. What tasks do you own? What does success look like? Better yet, propose your own ideas to your boss for what success in your role looks like! Identify an ambitious yet realistic door knocking target, for example, or the number of donations you want to personally bring in for the campaign." Keep a list of to dos so you can stay on top of key tasks and deadlines. If you mess up, be honest—don't tell co-workers first; go straight to your boss. Think of a way to solve the problem. People are rarely fired for trivialities and almost always get a second chance. "It's important to take ownership of your work," says Jessica Smith, former communications director for Senator Jim Webb. "Be responsive, give status updates to your boss, and don't leave at the end of the day without completing timely tasks."

Don't complain about projects given to you; just get them done. Jason Cabel Roe remembers, "It really is important that you take every assignment seriously. I was an intern at the Michigan Republican Party in 1993 and my boss gave me an assignment I thought was beneath me, so I didn't do what was asked. What I failed to realize is that it was a test of my ability and I failed. How can anyone expect you to handle big responsibilities if you don't do well with small ones?"

If you think you're unfairly being given too much or menial work, bring it up after a task is completed, not before. And don't question your boss in front of others; set aside some time to chat in private and keep the conversation professional, not personal.

Remember that your boss is not your friend—not on Facebook and not in real life. But your job is (at least partly) to make your boss' life easier and to make him or her look good. Be aware yet wary of internal power struggles. Every boss has something to prove as well; clue in to what they're dealing with.

A good manager can make a bad job tolerable, but a bad one can ruin a good job. A colleague of mine said, "There are no bad jobs just bad people." Try not to let unpleasant circumstances get you down, particularly during short-lived jobs like campaigns. Don't gossip about co-workers or your boss and never post anything negative online.

Finally, don't date co-workers—especially a boss or an intern (watch the movie *The Ides of March* and you'll understand why).

Relationships happen and hook-ups are common on campaigns, but it's a bad idea that can lead to drama and conflict. If there's something there, a real relationship can wait a few months. It's better to avoid, not contribute to, sexual harassment lawsuits and bad press. Your employer may even have a no-fraternization policy.

If You Do Get Fired

Take the high road, no matter how terrible or unwarranted the situation. Everyone has a long memory, and it's best to be known as a class act. If you get fired, thank your boss for the opportunity and ask for the terms of termination in writing, particularly if you're receiving severance or paid out vacation days. Don't bad mouth your boss or the organization, and don't do anything drastic, be it cutting off your hair or sending a tell-all email.

Christy Agner notes, "In politics, your reputation is all you have. You can't buy it. You can only earn it. And you can't get it back once it's gone."

If Your Boss Gets Fired

If your boss gets fired or leaves, you and your job may be vulnerable as well. Know your strengths (again, have them written out and quantified, if possible, ahead of time) and be prepared to essentially re-interview for your job with the new boss. On the other hand, especially in a fast-paced work environment, you may get a promotion or even take over for your boss when they get the boot, so be prepared to take on more responsibility.

Knowing It's Time to Leave

"Never stop shopping for jobs," notes campaign manager Adam Weiss. "Always be on the lookout for the next great opportunity." Sometimes a job has simply run its course. Don't stay in the comfort zone; if you're not being challenged it's time to look elsewhere. If your boss isn't going anywhere, co-workers don't pull their weight, the work culture isn't for you, the pace is frustrating, or your job responsibilities haven't increased in years, it's time to leave.

Be ready to walk out the door. Keep contacts, key work product, and any other non-proprietary documents on your personal computer or a flash drive. Never assume you'll have access to your work computer or email if you're fired or quit.

Firing is the more extreme form of pushing out. If you sense things aren't going well for you, think about leaving on your own terms before you're asked to leave.

Telling Your Boss That You're Leaving

If you're taking another position, don't tell your manager you're leaving until you have the offer in writing and have accepted it in writing as well. And always tell your boss first. It can be tempting to tell work friends about a secret job search, but resist the urge. Some people disagree with me on this and say that current co-workers can be helpful in your search. But only you know your own situation best—if you trust your co-workers, consider reaching out for help. I'd err on the side of caution and stay quiet until your new position is a done deal.

To help you leave on good terms, make sure to give proper notice, wrap up any ongoing work and leave an exit memo for your replacement, and perhaps, offer to meet the new staffer for lunch or a few hours of training. Remember, you want a good reference down the road, so make the transition as easy as possible.

The Political Ladder:
- ✓ Track your value throughout the year, not just before a review
- ✓ Project a can-do, get things done attitude
- ✓ Know what your "real" job is
- ✓ Don't date co-workers
- ✓ Always be ready to walk out the door
- ✓ Tell your manager first and leave on good terms

YOUR ONLINE PERSONA

In this day and age, the personal is public. Whether you like it or not, your online persona is part of your resume. Employers will check you out online, so make sure everything out there is job interview-ready. I've never used a paid site like Reputation.com, but it's pretty much built for people who are hyper-obsessed with their online persona. Political veteran Simone L. Ward says, "I have not hired people because of their online profiles. Once it's out there, it's out there. Abide by the old saying, 'If you don't want to see it on the front page *of The New York Times*, don't say it.' Same goes for if you have to ask, don't post it."

Google

Start off by Googling yourself to see what results pop up; if you have a common name, add some keywords (like former employers or your hometown) to narrow your search. You can also set up Google alerts for yourself (include any iteration of your name, such as common nicknames or your maiden name), so you know right away if someone has posted something new.

This is your first line of defense for awkward interview questions. Trust me – someone once blogged that I prevented a couple from getting milk for their baby at a political event (they were really trying to sneak backstage to meet John Edwards), which showed up in a Google search. I did get asked about it in a job interview, and luckily, I knew about the outrageous post ahead of time. Thanks to my handy Google alerts, I had my talking points ready!

Facebook

Oh, Facebook. So fun and yet so easy to get yourself into trouble. Even if your privacy settings are strict enough to prevent a future employer from seeing any unprofessional photos, be vigilant about checking and updating settings and about who you accept as friends. As with Google alerts, make sure you adjust your preferences so that you receive an email notification whenever anyone posts on your Wall or tags you in a photo, so you can check if it's appropriate right away.

But, and this is a big but, if you want to be super safe, take down or de-tag any embarrassing photos and read old Wall posts to ensure that Saturday night's shenanigans aren't broadcasted to the world. Politics is a small community and your future boss may know many of your friends—so those privacy settings may not be enough, after all. Employers expect you to have a life outside of the office, but they don't want you to be the poster girl or guy for spring break '07. And it goes without saying, but I'll say it anyway: take down anything offensive or illegal.

Your boss is not your friend – not in life, and not on Facebook. While many political workplaces encourage the use of personal social media networks to spread the word about events, issues, or fundraising deadlines, be careful about what else you post. I had an employee who was notorious for missing deadlines. One day, after missing a deadline on a key report, I saw a Facebook post about baseball on the staffer's wall – sent minutes ago, while at work. Needless to say, I was furious.

Unless you're working in a conservative environment, you likely don't need to erase your online persona or eliminate your personality altogether. Take a cue from co-workers or just ask HR if there is a set policy. Steer away from posting anything about work and never, ever post anything bad about your boss or co-workers.

Finally, don't friend people you don't know. No one likes a stalker.

LinkedIn

I love LinkedIn. It serves multiple functions, and unlike Facebook, it's not addictive and there's no need to check it every day.

LinkedIn is an extension of your resume. It's a place to talk about jobs in more depth, listing several bullets or being more descriptive about a particular role (you should still be concise and accomplishment-focused though). There is also room to list special skills and include a summary of your experience. Finally, it allows you to link to other sites, like Facebook, Twitter, YouTube or About.me.

Perhaps most importantly, LinkedIn allows others to recommend you. Recommendations can come from co-workers and peers, people you supervised, and people who supervised you. It's easy to ask for these recommendations once you build your network on the site. Potential employers may look at these mini-references before an interview, so choose recommenders wisely.

For LinkedIn to be truly effective, you need to maximize your contacts, or what the site calls connections. Users can upload contacts from email, connect through Facebook, and use past jobs to find connections. The more people you connect to, the more connections you can see down the line, which leads to . . . Best. Spy. Tool. Ever. LinkedIn allows you to see who you know, who *they* know, and where they all work and worked. Interviewing at an organization with which you're not familiar? Look up who you know there, or who can connect you to get the inside scoop. Found the person with your dream job? Look up their career path.

You can also sign up for Job Change Notifier (a separate application) to find out when a connection posts a new job or title. Talk about getting the inside track on job openings.

As part of your networking efforts, add every new connection to LinkedIn as soon as you meet them. Unlike Facebook, this is acceptable and encouraged. Think of it as exchanging business cards online.

About.me

A relatively new tool, About.me allows you to create a professional homepage. It's pretty basic – just a photo or background of your choosing, a bio, and links to other social media sites. But it's an easy, clean way to create a basic site about yourself and a way to publicize who you are and your accomplishments.

Twitter

Twitter is a great tool for keeping up with the political world and getting your name out there. To stay informed, follow relevant people in politics, experts on issues you care about, state politicians, and local bloggers. To further raise your profile, reply to tweets that peak your interest. However, don't go overboard replying to every comment and, like Facebook, beware the inappropriate tweet.

Twitter is also chock-full of insider news and gossip about campaigns and organizations. If you're in the interview process, be sure to follow some key staff ahead of time so you are up on any scoops.

It never hurts to build up your own following, too. This may prove handy once you land a job in politics.

Dating Websites

How awkward would it be for someone to recognize you from a dating website during a job interview? Exactly. For the time being, take down your profile.

Online Privacy at Work

Nothing at work is private, including your email, Gchats, AIMs, web browser history, phone logs – you name it. It is legal and par for the course for employers to read employee emails and any and all communication falls under campaign finance and coordination legalities. So watch what you put in writing in any format.

The Political Ladder:
- ✓ Google yourself and set up Google alerts
- ✓ Take down embarrassing photos and triple-check your privacy settings on Facebook
- ✓ Set up a LinkedIn account
- ✓ Use Twitter strategically to build up your name and get insider news
- ✓ Take down online dating profiles

CAMPAIGNS 101

While most political jobs are hectic, campaigns are even more intense. Media scrutiny and enormous amounts of money compound the problem. There are just some on-the-job situations that are unique to campaigns.

Justin Krebs, founder of Living Liberally says, "A campaign is a chance to be exhausted and exhilarated, to learn fast, to give your all and to know that on one certain day it either will or won't have worked." It's a high-stress, high-stakes situation unlike any other but with huge rewards — for you, your candidate, your party, and even your country.

Types of Campaigns

First, there are some basics to know about the different types and levels of campaigns, which include local, state, and national campaigns. Local races and state legislative campaigns can have only one or two staffers while statewide or national campaigns can have hundreds or thousands of employees. You'll learn a lot and wear many hats on a local campaign, and it's a great way to get your feet wet. But local races can be a closed, insiders-only club; it usually is personal and everyone knows everyone.

For state legislative races, the professionalism varies tremendously from state to state and race to race, depending on competitiveness. Statewide races and ballot measures as well as congressional races are (again, depending on their competitiveness) usually big budget operations with a professional staff structure. Off-year legislative races like New Jersey and Virginia, big city mayoral races, and down-ballot races in states like Iowa and New Hampshire (especially leading up to presidential primary season) may see an unusual amount of interest and outside money, as well.

Presidential campaigns feel like small start-ups in places like Iowa and New Hampshire or if you're working for a long-shot candidate. Be prepared to get laid off for several months between the end of the primary season and the beginning of the general election. Once a candidate becomes the presumptive nominee, get ready for layers of staff and bureaucracy, along with huge budgets that you'll never see a piece of unless you're a media consultant.

Being a Good Campaign Staffer

Campaign Life

For a humorous take on campaign life, search on YouTube for the Xtranormal cartoon, "So you want to work on campaigns?" It sums up what *not* to do. Yes, I'm serious. Go look it up. I'll wait.

Campaign staffers work hard and make little money. They subsist on pizza, donuts, and coffee. Campaigns may last just a few weeks or over a year, and the hours are long and unpredictable. You don't get holidays off (many a campaign staffer has spent Christmas in Iowa or New Hampshire), and coming in at 7 a.m. on a Saturday and working like it's a weekday is completely normal.

Working multiple campaign cycles is the fastest way to expand your skill set and move up the political career ladder. To ascend the ladder even faster be ready to pack up and move across the country at a moment's notice to work 16 hours per day and sleep on a stranger's couch. As Georgie Aguirre-Sacasa, chief of staff at America Votes, put it, "Who knew you could interview one day and move your whole life, not knowing anyone, to a new city the next." Or take this lesson from former hack Jonathan Lyons: "I drove to New Hampshire on January 1, 2004, to work for the Kerry campaign, with a spoken promise that a semi-paid internship was waiting for me when I got there. I think I found out the day before which office I was going to. I didn't know where I'd stay for the month or what I'd be doing. I just knew that I'd hit the big leagues, and I'd do anything necessary to stay there."

You may work for multiple campaigns in one cycle: it's a high turnover industry and sometimes you lose a primary or just don't mesh with your candidate or campaign manager. It's OK; future employers know that leaving a campaign may not be your fault or may be the result of extenuating circumstances.

You'll wear lots of hats – the job description doesn't begin to cover it. Be assertive and start wherever needed to get in the door. Campaign veteran Emmy Ruiz notes, "There's no unimportant job on a campaign but everyone starts off at the bottom of the totem pole. Volunteer if you need to, and you'll be hired when the campaign heats up and the budget expands." You have to go above and beyond to stand out; it may seem weird but you need to be a self-promoter and point out – subtly, or with humor – your accomplishments in order for them to be noticed. It may be necessary to ask for the more substantive work once you've proved yourself; people will assign tasks to whoever is closest to them. On campaigns, you're always in over your head – don't let it paralyze you, just get the work done.

Develop the skills everyone wants: web and social media, writing, fundraising, and databases for voter contact. "You don't want to be a jack-of-all-trades, master of none, as the saying goes," says political vet Tyler Mounsey. "Many political people are, and the truth is, you need to know a lot of different things to survive." More than anything else, a great attitude goes a long way. Do whatever is needed, whenever it needs to be done and you will go far in campaigns. "Never, ever go into a campaign and say, 'I think I would be great at policy. You know, writing white papers and being a spokesperson for the candidate,'" says political veteran Donnie Fowler. "You'll lose credibility immediately."

You can, however, move up incredibly fast if you work hard. Political operative Mike Shields took a pay cut for a crappy job at the Republican National Committee doing the clips (this was 1994 when there was no internet; he literally had to cut out newspaper articles with scissors, paste them to paper, and copy them for the staff). The first person in every day at 4 a.m., he also stayed late to learn how to write press releases. Seven months and another job later, he was offered a position as a spokesperson for then-Speaker of the House Newt Gingrich.

In a nutshell: hard work + dependability + loyalty + sense of humor + smarts = success.

Working with the Candidate

To be an effective staffer on a campaign, it's important to know how politicians think and what makes up their daily lives. They are often very smart and well-versed on issues. They are always busy, have fast-paced schedules, and must attend many events each day, including weekends. Many commute from their home districts to DC or the state capitol so personal and family time can be in very short supply. In sum, it can be tough to keep up. There's a reason these folks are at the pinnacle of power. As Hill and campaign veteran

Hayley Zachary says, "You are a reflection of your boss. Remember to uphold that standard at all times."

Campaign staffers must anticipate needs – even small things. As the assistant to the chairwoman of the Democratic Congressional Campaign Committee, I wasn't responsible for determining which races to target or raising money for candidates. I was responsible for helping the trains run on time and making the congresswoman's life easier. I always kept extra pantyhose in my purse. It wouldn't solve the world's problems, but it could solve hers.

The Fam (Theirs, Not Yours)

Politics is often a family affair (see: Kennedy, Bush, Clinton, Paul, Podesta, Brown, Meek, Sanchez….you get my gist). Kids of politicians and donors may get a foot in the door a little faster and a little higher up the ladder but often feel the need to prove themselves twice as hard. There's a lot of nepotism on both sides of the aisle. It's common to encounter a family member-as-staffer many times over the course of your political life. But the operations of a campaign should be left to professionals, not family or volunteers. While many family members can become professionals, maintain a healthy skepticism of any campaign with too many family members on staff.

On the other hand, family members can be a huge asset, even beyond smiling for the cameras. As a staffer, particularly one who frequently interacts with the candidate, keeping the spouse and family happy is part of the job. This doesn't mean delivering the weekly dry cleaning or putting together white papers on every obscure issue that arises. If you get frequent requests from a family member for work above and beyond, bring it up with your boss. But keep in mind that family members on a campaign are often under unwarranted and unaccustomed stress and scrutiny, so cut them a little slack; treat them with respect, and pay attention to the little things that can go a long way, like making sure the candidate's husband has water, too.

"Having been on both sides of this equation, I appreciate the delicate balance between keeping the family happy and not allowing your campaign to devolve into amateur hour," says Alicia Menendez, who worked on the race of her father, U.S. Senator Robert Menendez, and as a staffer on various statewide races. "One of our consultants reminded me that I had a role that no one else could play: daughter and confidante. She advised me to bring my campaign concerns and suggestions to the paid staff, but to refrain from bending my dad's ear. Setting clear expectations of roles and boundaries as early as possible helps avoid unnecessary drama."

Once You Hit the Ground

Bad Management Practices

Campaigns are not known for good management. There's no human resources department to deal with logistics or keep staff in check. People are often promoted because they were good at their previous job or they happened to be on a winning campaign (and were able to take credit for the win), not because they have any people skills or experience managing big teams effectively. With such short timelines and limited budgets, campaigns also don't focus on staff training. Instead, there's a natural ladder people climb after they have put in their time because there's simply not enough good campaign staff. Throw in prickly personalities and weeks if not months on end of bad food and not enough sleep, and it's a recipe for personnel disaster.

The best advice I can give is to be prepared and try not to take anything personally. People don't always mesh well under the best of circumstances, much less in a campaign scenario. Future political employers know what this kind of workplace environment is like and won't be shocked if you comment that it isn't the lifestyle for you or if you delicately answer why your campaign boss isn't listed as a reference.

So, expect yellers, work-a-holics, bosses who sleep until noon and don't get fired, martyrs, and no positive feedback. Hopefully you'll be pleasantly surprised. If someone crosses an obvious line though, such as sexual harassment or bullying, tell your boss, your boss' boss, or the campaign lawyer or chairperson.

Getting Layered

Towards the end of a campaign, you're (hopefully) organizing yourself out of a job. As more people come in, your area of responsibility shrinks; there's so much to do and the more hands, the better. This is a good thing, and it's not a reflection of your work. Everyone gets layered (see Glossary), even campaign managers and state directors. But sometimes this occurs a little earlier than you'd like or an adversarial relationship develops. This may happen when a perceived "outsider" comes in, like a DC operative or a staffer for a former primary opponent. Remember that everyone is working towards the same goal – winning – and try to make the best of it.

Know who you're working with. The disheveled, unshaven guy who comes in for the last month of the campaign is likely a major political player who can help you down the road. We call them "ubers" – very senior, established politicos who come in to help a campaign for a few weeks or several months (see Glossary). Often, ubers go to the same districts or states cycle after cycle. They may have cut their teeth working for the governor or a former senator. They usually know what they're talking about and have a lot to teach, so pay attention and learn from the best.

Not Your Backyard

First, if you're the layeree (a new word I invented), buy their love. Beer, pizza, donuts, whatever; trust me, it works. I showed up to work in Green Bay, Wisconsin, in October 2004 with a box of donuts and it helped break the ice. Also recognize that, as the newbie, you need to prove yourself and earn the trust of the staff.

When taking a job in a brand new place, it's important to understand regional issues and ideology. It's all too easy to ignore local issues – ideological, personal and otherwise – when it's not your backyard. Railing against coal in West Virginia, bad-mouthing your Ford rental car in Michigan, complaining about corn subsidies in Iowa, and making fun of tree-huggers in Oregon are all great ways to get fired. Also, know who makes up the "base" of the state's voters and volunteers. For Democrats, it's important to know that college elites and labor guys don't speak the same language; same for Wall Street suits and Tea Party activists on the Republican side.

"Take the time to learn the local culture," notes consultant Jennie Blackton, who has worked in local races across the country. "Make an effort to learn how locals communicate. Talk to the grocery store clerk and the cab driver; find out what's really bothering them about their community. Look around Main Street and see which businesses are hurting. Collect anecdotes from them about what would really help and fold that into the candidate's communications strategy."

If you're unfamiliar with a community, be careful who you primary. Understand the impact, especially if you're young or from out of state. Know when you're taking on The Establishment – sometimes it's a wonderful and necessary thing and sometimes it comes back to bite you. Again, politics is a small world.

Finally, learn to tolerate the crazies. The candidate, staff, and other volunteers need to put up with them for years to come. So find a less relevant task for them to do and try to limit debate time until after nightly reports are submitted.

There IS Such a Thing as Bad Press

Never, ever talk to the press without permission; doing so is a sure-fire way to get fired on a campaign. Off the record, on background, whatever – the only people who should talk to the press are the communications staff. Also be aware of airing dirty laundry in public. "You never know who is sitting next to you in open spaces," says online strategist Erin Hofteig. "Do not say anything you wouldn't want repeated back to you." This goes double for state capitols and in Washington, DC, where the woman on a park bench, next to you on the metro, or two stools over at the bar could be a political reporter. It happens, even to people who know better. So don't let it happen to you.

And, as campaign operative Anne Johnson reminds us, "It's campaign 101: first do no harm."

Don't Go To Jail

Know the law. Arm yourself with enough information to know the difference between people and situations that are acceptable and those that are sketchy—when in doubt, ask the campaign lawyer. Cash contributions that aren't counted, stealing yard signs, no "paid for by" on communications – these illegal acts happen frequently, and often by accident, on campaigns.

A common conundrum is whether staff can and should vote in the state or district in which they are working, since they may be on the ground for months or even a year. Jackie Bray, who has worked on campaigns all over the country, notes, "On the one hand you are living in that state. On the other hand, especially on high profile campaigns, you'll be held to a higher standard, one that isn't only about the letter of the law but about the optics, how things look. When in doubt ask a lawyer, but be careful. Your voter protection staff has a job to do and it isn't keeping you out of trouble. Find a lawyer who is barred in the state in which you are working with experience on these issues, and rely on his or her advice."

And don't try to cut corners – you may do something badly or even illegally. Better to get fired than go to jail.

Your Personal Life

The truth is, you won't really have much of a personal life while working on a campaign. Here are some general tips for keeping yours in order based on way too many lessons I learned the hard way:

- Make time to exercise and eat well – at least until the last few weeks or Get Out The Vote (GOTV).
- Sleep as much as you can, when you can.
- Don't live with co-workers. It's an all-consuming life already and everyone needs a break. (On the other hand, this can be a great bonding experience.)
- Drink with people after hours but don't get too drunk.
- Always be honest with numbers – how many doors knocked, how much money raised, how many attendees at the rally – both internally and externally.
- Try to maintain outside friendships, even if it's just an occasional check-in phone call to keep you grounded. Your non-political friends don't care what you do, so don't try to convince them. They won't understand why you missed their Columbus Day weekend wedding, but hopefully they will forgive you.
- Plan your finances. Arrange for auto-pay on as many things as possible and put everything else on your calendar several days before due dates to avoid skipping a payment. You're not making much money, but there's no need to simultaneously ruin your credit, too.

In the Meantime...

Campaigns are go-go-go all the time for weeks, months, even years. It takes a while to come down off that high, win or lose. There's a lot of downtime between campaigns. It can be frustrating and even depressing to be unemployed for a long time and then potentially go through rounds of disappointment when trying to find your next job. Former campaigner Nick Warshaw points out, "Many of my bosses have helped me obtain my next position through their connections. When serving on campaigns, it's easier to solicit help from a boss, because the campaign has a defined end date and, as such, everyone on a campaign is looking for a job." Don't send your resume out until after Election Day. But (wink wink) it's a good idea to start sending campaign updates to friends before then.

"Whether you're at the bottom of the rung on the field team or rubbing elbows with your candidate as part of the finance operation, do your best to get to know everyone in your organization and stay connected to it," says Keya Dannenbaum, co-founder and CEO of Elect Next. "They're going to scatter to the political winds once the campaign is over, and you never know who may end up helping you or who you may end up helping down the road."

Unemployment insurance is a godsend. Employers pay it even if you don't collect, so take advantage and pay the rent. Research unemployment benefits in your state during the campaign so you can file as soon as you're eligible. Periods of unemployment can be a good time to hone your skills, too. Services like PoliTemps are helpful for finding temporary work. Don't be afraid to ask non-political friends for short-term projects, and no one will fault you for taking a holiday season retail job or tending bar for a while.

And, chances are, a lot of your political friends will be in the same boat. So enjoy those mid-day movies and the empty gym. Make your employed friends buy the next round; you can return the favor later.

The Political Ladder:
✓ Think about the type of campaign you want to work on
✓ Take care of your personal life
✓ Research unemployment before Election Day so you can file right away

The Political Ladder

Prepare
- ✓ Identify any needs and wants
- ✓ Make a list of important skills
- ✓ Do your salary math
- ✓ Google yourself and set up Google alerts for your name
- ✓ Take down embarrassing photos and triple-check your privacy settings on Facebook
- ✓ Set up a LinkedIn account
- ✓ Use Twitter strategically to build up your name
- ✓ Take down online dating profiles
- ✓ Set up RSS feeds and follow Twitter accounts for companies, organizations, and candidates you're interested in working for
- ✓ Get business cards printed
- ✓ Buy thank you notes
- ✓ Invest in business attire clothing, if needed, for interviews

Current College Students
- ✓ Take Economics
- ✓ Make your mark through school or extracurriculars
- ✓ Get some real world experience

Career Switchers
- ✓ Set realistic expectations for salary and title
- ✓ Go on lots of informational interviews

Network
- ✓ Make a list of contacts and track them in a spreadsheet
- ✓ Go to as many political events as possible
- ✓ Use trainings as networking opportunities
- ✓ Find a mentor

Get Ready

- ✓ Write and practice your "60-second spot"
- ✓ Contact former bosses and co-workers as needed to help you craft accomplishment-driven bullets for your resume
- ✓ Have a non-political and a political friend review your resume
- ✓ Create a perfect, triple spell-checked generic resume
- ✓ Create a perfect, triple spell-checked generic cover letter
- ✓ Make a list of potential references with current contact information
- ✓ Compile possible writing samples or create new ones to showcase relevant skills
- ✓ Write down answers to likely interview questions

For Campaigns

- ✓ Think about the type of campaign you want to work on
- ✓ Get your personal life and finances in order
- ✓ Research unemployment in the state in which you're working, so you can file as soon as you're eligible

GLOSSARY

A lot of being an insider is knowing the terminology. The political world has a ton of acronyms, abbreviations, and slang.

Below is my not-even-close-to-exhaustive dictionary of terms I use in the book. There's also a fun list on Daily Kos: http://www.dailykos.com (keep in mind, I've never heard of half of the terms they list but many are relevant). There are many other books and websites as well; just Google political slang, jargon, and abbreviations.

Party Committees

DNC – Democratic National Committee (DNC); sometimes called the Dink

DGA – Democratic Governors Association (DGA)

DSCC – Democratic Senatorial Campaign Committee (DSCC); often called the DS

DCCC – Democratic Congressional Campaign Committee (DCCC); often called the D-Trip

DLCC – Democratic Legislative Campaign Committee (DLCC)

RNC – Republican National Committee (RNC)
RGA – Republican Governors Association (RGA)
NRSC – National Republican Senatorial Committee (NRSC)
NRCC – National Republican Campaign Committee (NRCC)
RLCC – Republican Legislative Campaign Committee (RLCC)

Political Terminology

The Base or Base Vote – Voters most likely to support your party/ campaign. For Democrats, this often refers to African-Americans, Latinos, youth, unmarried women, and labor. For Republicans, this usually refers to white, evangelical, and/or rural voters.

Cycles – Used to describe the length of time of a campaign; for instance 2009-2010 is one campaign cycle, culminating with the November 2010 election.

GOTV – Get Out The Vote; refers to the end of a campaign when you switch from persuading voters to simply making sure your supporters actually turn out.

Hacks – People who move from place to place each election cycle, working on whatever campaign comes their way.

The Hill – Refers to Capitol Hill, where the Capitol Building and congressional offices are located; also a political newspaper and online publication.

GLOSSARY

Layered — When someone comes in a rung above you or at the same level on a campaign with the same basic job responsibilities. The layeree (a word I invented) is the person who gets layered.

Politico — Someone who works in politics; also a political newspaper and online publication.

Ubers — Very senior, established politicos who come in to help a campaign for a few weeks or several months.

White paper — In-depth position papers on an issue, often used in conjunction with other press materials to provide additional background information.

Wonks — Thinkers who like debating policy questions.

HELP FOR JOB SEEKERS

Websites

Democratic GAIN: democraticgain.org
Extensive resources for job seekers; Republicans, hold your nose, and use the examples anyway!

George Washington University Graduate School of Political Management: gspm.org/jobs
List of Washington, DC-focused political job sites.

The Google Resume, Behavioral Preparation Grid: thegoogleresume.com/sample-materials.html.
Help for answering likely interview questions about how you handle various situations.

The Management Center: managementcenter.org/resources
Tools for managers as well as employees.

Political Job Hunt: politicaljobhunt.com
Job search site from the creator of Taegan Goddard's Political Wire.

Books

Career Opportunities in Politics, Government, and Activism by Joan Axelrod-Contrada
This book describes various types of jobs, from U.S. Representative to Consumer Activist to City Assessor. It includes salary ranges, tips for entry, and appendices such as graduate school programs and advocacy groups.

An Insider's Guide to Political Jobs in Washington by William T. Endicott
A helpful overview of federal government jobs and campaigns, particularly a breakdown of Congressional and Executive Branch Jobs, this book also includes short "case studies"/ biographies of top Republican and Democratic politicos.

Job Interviews for Dummies by Joyce Lain Kennedy
Part of the famous *Dummies* series, this book discusses interview how-tos in a fun, engaging way.

The Google Resume by Gayle Laakmann McDowell
My friend Gayle's top-selling book includes helpful, cross-industry tips.

Managing to Change the World: The Nonprofit Leader's Guide to Getting Results by Allison Green and Jerry Hauser
Excellent advice, including worksheets and how tos for both managers and employees.

The 250 Job Interview Questions You'll Most Likely Be Asked by Peter Veruki
This book has good interview prep tips with sample questions and answers.

The Plum Book (United States Government Policy and Supporting Positions)
The Bible of government jobs, this lists all Executive Branch political jobs.

FURTHER READING

This is by no means a comprehensive list, but it includes great political books recommended by friends and former co-workers.

Showdown at Gucci Gulch: Lawmakers, Lobbyists, and the Unlikely Triumph of Tax Reform by Jeffrey Birnbaum and Alan Murray

The Years of Lyndon Johnson by Robert A. Caro (three-part series)

Alexander Hamilton by Ron Chernow

What It Takes by Richard Ben Cramer

Call the Briefing by Marlin Fitzwater

The Survivor by John F. Harris

Game Change by John Heilemann and Mark Halperin

Primary Colors: A Novel of Politics by Joe Klein

All's Fair by Mary Matalin and James Carville

Hardball by Chris Matthews

John Adams by David McCullough

Truman by David McCullough

Smashmouth by Dana Milbank

The Audacity to Win by David Plouffe

All Too Human by George Stephanopoulos

The Making of the President 1960 by Theodore H. White

The Agenda by Bob Woodward

19420056R00078

Made in the USA
Lexington, KY
17 December 2012